An At[...]

Mee[...]

by

Phillip H. Krapf

Origin Press
SAN RAFAEL, CA

Origin Press

PO Box 151117 • San Rafael, CA 94915
888.267.4446 • originpress.com

Origin Press is a division of Wisdom Media LLC
wisdommedia.us

Copyright © 2008 by Phil Krapf

All rights reserved. No part of this book may be reproduced in any manner whatsoever without prior written permission from the publisher, except for quotations embodied in critical articles or reviews.

Cover design by Phillip Dizick
pdizick@earthlink.net

Publisher's Cataloging-in-Publication
(Provided by Quality Books, Inc.)

Krapf, Phillip H.
 Meetings with Paul : an atheist discovers his guardian angel / by Phillip H. Krapf.
 p. cm.
 Includes index.
 LCCN: 2008926737
 ISBN-13: 978-1-57983-021-2
 ISBN-10: 1-57983-021-8

 1. Guides (Spiritualism) 2. Guardian angels.
 3. Krapf, Phillip H.   I. Title. II. Title: Atheist discovers his guardian angel.

BF1275.G85K73 2008   133.9
                          QBI08-600092

First printing May 2008
10 9 8 7 6 5 4 3 2 1

Printed in the United States of America

Table of Contents

Author's Preface vi
Foreword by Timothy Wyllie ix
A Note to the Reader xvi

1. Telepathic Summons 1
2. Our Paths Cross 14
3. A Paradox of Terms 21
4. Angels Aren't Perfect 32
5. The Nature of the Job 40
6. The Big Question 49
7. My Hero 57
8. Times Were Good 66
9. Dirty Linen 73
10. Shades of Rod Serling 78
11. Precocious Child 98
12. Testing Paul 127
13. Opening Communication 148
14. Contact 163
15. Lonesome Journey 172
16. The Cargo Cult 191
17. Occasional Visitor 200

Epilogue 203
Postscript: An Update on the Contract Project . . 214

Author's Preface

It might seem devilishly ironic that on an Easter Sunday I should meet a man who claims to be my guardian angel. But I can't think of any other day that would be more appropriate, even for a lifelong atheist.

At the time of our initial meeting, Paul was merely a mysterious stranger with whom I crossed paths at a public park in Pinole, California, on the morning of Sunday, April 4, 1999. And I wouldn't learn of our special relationship until nine months later.

That occurred when I unexpectedly came face to face with him for the second time in January of 2000. I accepted the circumstances and nature of our bond with a mixture of reactions, not the least of which were astonishment and a certain guarded skepticism. I never had given serious consideration to the existence of such supernatural or metaphysical entities, if indeed that's what he was.

I had introduced Paul in a book I wrote shortly afterward as a peripheral character who had entered my life quite strangely and suddenly. It is not necessary for the reader to know the details of those events in order to understand and follow this narrative. But for those who are curious and interested in learning more about the foundation of our relationship, they can refer to my previous two books, *The Contact Has Begun* and *The Challenge of Contact*.

Nearly two years passed after our second meeting before I saw him again. That began a series of sessions in which we met dozens and dozens of times, beginning in November of 2001. It was a magical chapter in my life, filled with soul-searching (in a generic rather that a spiritual or religious sense) revelations, periods of gut-busting laughter, ethereal moments of penetrating introspection, and a rich treasure trove of discoveries that opened doors to a fertile wonderland of mind and spirit that I had never before explored. This newly discovered aspect of my life apparently has been a part of my makeup since the early days of my coming into this world, and yet I had never been conscious of it. I was somewhat surprised.

Although it was late in my life when I became aware of Paul's existence—I was sixty-three at the time—he claims that he has been my constant companion for a lifetime. We not only have had some grand adventures together, but he also helped me to relive many significant moments of my past in which he played a major role, though I was unaware of that fact at the time. And from that discovery I gained consciousness-raising insight and came away with a most precious gift—a deeper understanding of who I am.

I began writing this narrative while still harboring reservations about certain aspects of it. But I thought that if I voiced those uncertainties, questions, and challenges as the issues arose, it could seriously interfere with the smooth flow of the account herein, and become annoyingly intrusive or even unfair to the reader. So I decided to put aside my natural tendency to quibble and to instead let readers draw their own conclusions, with at least the intention of not imposing myself into the picture.

I thought then, and still believe now, that a critical analysis of those areas that gave me pause could be undertaken at a more opportune time. So for now I have attempted to relate the story as accurately and objectively as I could, and in the frame of mind of someone who accepts his experiences as they happened and takes them at face value. That is, I took aim at that goal, to the degree that I was capable: to become strictly a narrator and describe the material—facts, statements, conclusions, observations, et cetera—as it was presented and happened to me, whether or not I unqualifiedly accepted it all or felt that certain portions required further serious discussion.

I must emphasize that I have *tried* to maintain a certain narrative neutrality, but have not completely succeeded. I gave it my best shot, at least.

Join me now as I retrace the path of this remarkable journey.

>Phillip H. Krapf
>Valencia, California
>March 2008

Foreword

I found myself approaching Phillip Krapf's new book somewhat cautiously, since I was almost certain his understanding of guardian angels would turn out to be different from mine.

I have known Phil ever since the late 1990s when I contacted him after reading his first book, *The Contact Has Begun*. A number of idiosyncratic details in this book's account of his meetings with a group of extraterrestrials he calls the Verdants rang true to me and corroborated some of my own researches.

In a field in which there are likely more frauds and poseurs than there are genuine contactees, Phil's encounters with the Verdants and his obvious sincerity and confusion in the face of extraterrestrial expectations all struck a familiar note. Despite its outrageous aspects, I could sense the truth in his claim of a pending extraterrestrial intervention.

Meeting Phil and getting to know him over the years has confirmed my original intuition. He is possibly the least likely person I could ever imagine who would fabricate either his encounters with ETs, or his later meetings with his guardian angel. Indeed, his skepticism and constant self-questioning run like a gradually diminishing stream throughout this book.

And perhaps that is exactly the way it is intended to be.

If a hard-nosed, atheistic, newspaperman can find himself thrown into such extraordinary circumstances, then there really is hope for everybody.

So, why the caution?

Having experienced a brief glimpse of my own guardian angels in the course of a Near Death Experience in 1973 as well as extensive *internal* contact with one of them from 1983 to the present day, I find it immediately challenging to believe that Paul actually appears to Phil in a material body—a body that can deliver Phil a bear hug and yet, mysteriously, leaves no indentation when sitting on the edge of a bed; Paul possesses an apparently physical vehicle that can appear solid to Phil and yet be simultaneously invisible to others.

Apart from the few references in the Bible, I know of no authentic contemporary account that speaks of guardian angels as physical presences. As far as I have been led to understand, angels choose to stay concealed from us on a slightly higher frequency than our physical senses are tuned to. They say they do this as much for our benefit as their own, so that we do not become overly reliant on them and relinquish our freedom of choice by giving over our personal power to them.

Yet here is Phillip Krapf, an atheist and self-proclaimed skeptic, a man I know and have come to trust, having scores of such meetings. How could this be possible? I'd been in contact with him intermittently throughout this period and yet I never caught even a hint of these meetings with Paul. In fact, since our mutual interest was the Verdants, I now find it ironic that I had tended to steer clear of the subject of angels over the course of our discussions.

Of course I was delighted when I finally heard some years later that he had met his angel, but as I said I was a little nervous too. I had witnessed some of the stress and disappointment Phil went through after the 9/11 attack and the Verdants' subsequent decision to withdraw from contact with Earth as reported in Phil's second book, *The Challenge of Contact*. I had to consider the possibility that a desperately distraught man might have concocted an "imaginary friend" to fill the hole left by his extraterrestrial friends. But even children know their imaginary friends are not real. And so it went, back and forth . . . It was with these thoughts and preconceptions that I started reading *Meetings with Paul*.

I wasn't far into the book before I realized how I had fallen foul of that very human proclivity to judge other people's experiences in the light of one's own.

As in his previous books, I could tell immediately that Phil was reporting his astonishing meetings with as much honesty and detail as he was capable. I knew what a realist he is and respected his constant attempts to get Paul to account for himself. I was also aware of what he had endured at the hands of cynical disbelievers in his Verdant encounters. It was impossible to seriously consider that he would want to go through that all over again, unless he had become utterly convinced in the authenticity of what he was experiencing.

I simply had to let go of my preconceptions and open my heart and mind to Phil's unfolding story.

Over the centuries, so many improbable fantasies and imagined opinions about angels have been floating around, that meeting Paul in the book cast for me a delightfully fresh and lucid light on the nature of guardian angels. It was not at all what I'd come to think, and yet with the same unmistakable resonance that had become familiar in my own relationship with Joy, the more talkative of my two companion angels.

I found that Paul's words and insights invariably rang true to my heart. Although I experience my own angels in perhaps a more spiritual context than Phil does, Paul's counsel broadly resonated with what I have been able to learn from my own angels.

However, this sort of contact is of necessity a very personal affair. Accepting the existence of beings so close to us that they know the innermost secrets of our psyches is challenging, to say the least. Frankly, it was something of a relief to learn from Paul that angels turn away from some of the most intimate details of our lives.

In a very valuable contribution to our understanding of the human/angel relationship, Paul talks at some length about the subtle balance required for guiding their human wards through their life lessons. And Phil, in his turn, discovers through direct experience what it is like to live for a few weeks without his angel's small, everyday interventions.

Angels, I believe, serve the *Atman*, the indwelling God in each of us, whether we believe in this God or not. They will guide us into those human experiences we need in order to grow in Spirit, whether or not we actually believe in Spirit. Sometimes they will present us with challenges that under normal conditions we would be too timid to take on. Phil's tale of his coming to terms with his childhood fears is a good example of this.

Facing up to our deepest fears; dealing with our early imprints; releasing all the reasons we deem ourselves of being unworthy of an angel's attention; and growing in real self-confidence—these things expand our potential to make contact with our angels. Yet we all experience this contact in different ways. And what is most important, there is no one right way.

Although I, too, started my search as an atheist, I had been involved in spiritual work for more than twenty years before I met my angels. The Phillip Krapf I have come to know was, in many ways, starting from square one. He is trying to deal with his atheism *while* he is talking with his angel.

One has to admire Paul's patience. Yet, given the urgency of the world situation, might there not be a clue in this? An implied message from the Unseen World?

Help, I believe they are saying, is truly close at hand to those bold and curious enough to entertain the reality of other dimensions of existence.

Those who are familiar with Phil's previous two books will appreciate the struggles that he had in coming to terms with his encounters with the Verdants. That Phil Krapf even survived that unfortunate ordeal without his Spirit being crushed, without becoming completely disillusioned with the spiritual dimensions of life, is a tribute both to his character and to the apparent beneficence of those very spiritual dimensions he so personally doubts.

Whether Paul ultimately turns out to be what he says he is, a guardian angel, or whether he is a Verdant masquerading as an angel—or, even an externalized projection of Phil's subconscious mind—isn't really the point. It is the effect Paul has on Phil that is important; it's the humor with which Paul handles Phil's truculence; and it's the wisdom Paul shows in encouraging Phil to make his own mistakes and learn from them.

We all have our doubts and worries. Nobody wants to be fooled in this most delicate of areas. Yet the angels always insist that we trust our finer feelings—our intuition.

Whether you, the reader, are an atheist or a believer, it is with your intuition that you will hear the deeper truths in this fascinating and provocative book. Read it with an open heart and mind. It is a profound gift to know that angels are only a heartbeat away, whether they appear—like Paul—in the physical, or whether they remain a purely interior experience.

The truth carries a quality, a certain tone or feeling, that we can all recognize when we hear it, see it, or read it. So, perhaps, the most important single contribution this book makes is that it opens the window to the *reality* of angels: We would recognize angels as solid and real presences, if we, too, could but perceive them.

If there is one thing I have learned from my own contact with the angelic realms over the years, it is to remain open to all celestial possibilities. At this delicate stage of human development, anything is truly possible.

    Timothy R. Wyllie
    New Mexico
    March, 2008

A Note to the Reader

I did not take notes, nor did I use a recording device, during any of the conversations that I have related in this book. As such, the material in quotation marks is not a verbatim account of what was spoken, but rather an approximation—a paraphrasing, if you will. I could not imagine writing the book without dialogue, which can be a valuable literary tool in providing drama, building characters, and giving the reader a sense of being included as an eavesdropper to the conversations as they took place.

While the quotations are not exact duplications of the actual words spoken, I have been as diligent as I possibly could to ensure that the quoted material accurately reflects the gist of what was said, the nuances behind the words. The dialogue is a fair representation of the emotions and thoughts of the speakers, free of bias or distortion, even though in most cases the phrasing is not a word for word account.

I think the dialogue adds much to the telling of the story. I hope you, the reader, agree.

Finally, names have been changed to protect the anonimity of the real persons being described. Paul's name has not been changed.

Phil Krapf

a telepathic summons

I grimaced as a shot of pain ripped through my abdomen, almost buckling my knees. This had gone on long enough; it was time to deal with my malady. I had been busy for several years speaking to groups after the publication of my first book in 1998, and the travel was taking its toll. The pain was getting worse by the week because of the long periods of time I was spending on my feet. Finally I took time out in November of 2001 to have the rupture surgically repaired.

The staples were removed on November 13 and I retired to my home to recuperate for a few days. I was anxious to begin my daily jogging regimen again, which had been put on hold for the surgery.

It all started the next day, my sixty-seventh birthday, as I settled in with a book in the afternoon. About 5:30 or 6:00 p.m.—it was already dark outside—I found myself reading the same paragraph over and over without comprehension.

When I became conscious of what was occurring, I concentrated on my state of mind and soon discovered that something was distracting me, although I wasn't quite sure if it was internal or external. I turned my full attention to listening for any noises—a dripping faucet, a humming motor from an appliance, the rhythmic thumping of a basketball by the neighbor boys outside my window.

I couldn't pinpoint it from my chair, but it had become an itch—almost on a subliminal level—that begged to be scratched. I put aside the book and embarked upon a search to see if I could discover the source, which by now had been transformed from a mere distraction to a full-blown beckoning of sorts. Something real was calling me, and my curiosity would not allow me to resist its lure. Although I didn't know where I was going or why, with a single-mindedness of purpose I walked out through the garage, around the side of the house, and into the back yard.

The motion-detector lights flashed on when I stepped outside, illuminating the yard, the barbecue area, and the gazebo, and that's when I spotted a dark figure, half-hidden in the shadows, sitting calmly in the gazebo. I was startled because no one should have been there, and his presence should have triggered the security lights but hadn't.

A medium-security prison is only several miles away and there have been several breakouts during the time I have lived in the area, which resulted each time in increased police activity. Racing police cars with sirens wailing and circling helicopters that thump the air and sweep the landscape with powerful searchlights are not easily ignored. During those events I tended to pay a bit more attention to access points to my property, specifically fences, gates, windows, and doors.

I don't know what caused me to be so brash, even foolhardy, because normally I am rather judicious in dealing with potentially dangerous situations. I'm not the type who goes looking for fights or confrontations, but under certain circumstances I can be just as impetuous as the next person. I marched straight toward the gazebo and the stranger to determine what he was doing on my property, quite prepared for a showdown if it came to that.

I was no more than ten feet away when a column of flame, at least two feet high, leaped from the fire pit, casting a great light upon the scene and filling in the deep shadows that had obscured the inside of the gazebo. The fire pit is fed by a natural gas line, and a standard gas fireplace key must be used to activate the valve on the concrete floor of the structure. In other words, it takes some movement, some bending, to reach the valve and use the key to open it so gas flows into the pit. And then the fuel must be ignited manually with a match or other open flame. I saw none of that activity precede the ignition of the gas. It had burst into flames almost as if on command.

By the light of the flame, which had settled down to a normal size, I saw his face clearly. The figure was wearing a grin that seemed big and bright enough to be seen in total darkness—almost as a bioluminescence—like a disembodied white gash in the blackness of night. I recognized him immediately.

It was Paul, my purported guardian angel. More than two years earlier, when I had first met him, he had been dressed casually in jeans, with a plaid shirt under his windbreaker, and white athletic shoes. He had looked to be in his forties, with a chiseled face and a full head of brown hair that stirred in the breeze. His eyes were an undistinguished, everyday blue.

Here he was again, still dressed in blue jeans, but the rustic look of the plaid shirt had given way to an open-collar dress shirt under a sport coat. The athletic shoes had been replaced by a handsome pair of cowboy boots (though I would have bet just about anything that they were fashioned from synthetic material rather than leather).

He got up and approached me with outstretched arms, the huge smile still on his face. I stuck out a hand of greeting, which he took, but he also pulled me into a tight bear hug. I'm not big on hugging men, but I endure it when others less inhibited embrace me. (When it comes to returning the hugs of women who are so inclined, I am not so reluctant—quite the opposite, I must admit.)

We greeted each other enthusiastically and slapped each other on the back in a display of masculinity that was, at least in my case, an awkward counterpoint to the hug. The heat given off by the flames dancing up through the layers of lava rocks felt good against the chill of the night air as I took a seat opposite him. The gazebo is one of my favorite places, day or night, but it is particularly enjoyable to sit quietly there in front of the fire after dark, while gazing upon the lights of the valley spreading out below.

I didn't even ask about the ignition of the fire pit, assuming that I couldn't even begin to fathom the mystical feats that angels can perform.

Paul seems to have a knack for reading my mind, but then again anyone could have done so simply by seeing the questioning expression plastered all over my mug.

"You're feeling confused, but don't be alarmed," he said. "In fact, your reaction is a good indication that you may have the gift."

That's another one of Paul's tedious traits, I would learn as time went by—jumping into a conversation as though I could read *his* mind, as though no matter what outlandish or esoteric statement he uttered, I would be in sync with him. I didn't know what he was talking about. What was this about a "gift"?

But I let that slide for the moment. There were more immediate issues to tackle.

"What are you doing here?" I exclaimed as we settled down before the fire. "I knew something was going on; something was bugging me and I couldn't concentrate on my reading."

"I was just calling you outside," he responded. "It was a psychic signal and some people do find it disconcerting at times. Others, however, are entranced and mesmerized by it—they find it soothing and comforting."

As was often the case—something else I would learn over time—Paul was far ahead in the conversation while I was still trying to get a handle on the preliminaries. He had mentioned a psychic signal and had moved on as though he were talking about something as prosaic as the price of gasoline and simply assumed that no explanation was necessary. Well, it was. When I don't understand something, I have to ask questions, to get clarification. If I don't stop the conversation at that point, then I'm totally lost after four or five more sentences.

"Wait. You're going too fast. Tell me about psychic signals," I said.

Paul replied that a psychic signal is merely something in the nature of a low-level telepathic communication that is quite vague.

Silly me, how come I didn't already know that?

According to Paul, there are several levels of telepathic signals. They range in power and clarity from the indeterminate type that I purportedly received, up to the highest level, in which the recipient "hears" the signal or message as clearly as if he or she were speaking face to face with the sender. And there are several midlevel ranges between the two extremes.

In my case, the imprecise signal merely got my attention in much the same way a person might whistle to summon a dog. At the highest level, I would have heard Paul's voice beckon me to the gazebo. I never determined whether I would have heard the voice silently in my head or as actual sound through my auditory system.

He was assuming a lot, I thought. I couldn't imagine that there was any real guarantee that I would be aware of such psychic signals, if there even were such things. But he said he was prepared to ring the doorbell as a last resort.

I suggested that he not beat around the bush in the future with such inexact signals, and that he get right to the point with a loud, clear, and unmistakable communication. Letting me know precisely where he was and what he wanted, I told him, was preferable to being led all over the house snooping in various corners, closets, and crannies on some elusive hunch.

Or at least ring the doorbell.

He took my little moment of pique to suggest that "some people react moodily to the psychic signal."

Had I just been zinged? Before I could react, he proceeded smoothly to address my suggestion.

"Eventually a direct communication can happen," he said, "but at the moment you have not achieved the ability to receive such messages."

Now *there* was an intriguing statement that begged for elaboration. However, Paul was not going to provide it without some prompting. I didn't hesitate to haul him right back to the subject when I realized that his line of conversation was headed off into the distance and not in the direction of clarification or explanation.

"Whoa, whoa! Back up a minute. I need special abilities? And how do I get them?"

I had never believed in telepathy. I always thought of it as an amusing and entertaining concept dreamed up by writers of fantasy adventures, stage magicians, and televangelists. Now, however, I was on the cusp of at least giving it serious consideration. After all, as reported in a previous book of mine, several years earlier I had followed a relentless "hunch" that had taken me 350 miles up the California coast to the small bedroom community of Pinole where Paul and I had first come face to face. I was told at that time that I had indeed been summoned telepathically, which I had suspected, all the while trying to deny such a notion. And there also was no denying that mere minutes earlier, I had felt a definite, if inscrutable, force of some sort that had drawn me from the house to the backyard to once again meet up with Paul. Some people might call it a psychic force, but I was more comfortable thinking of it as a hunch.

Characterizing those two events as anything more than mere coincidence was a struggle for this skeptic who always looks for a rational, materialistic explanation of seemingly mysterious phenomena. Many people would have no problem viewing them as obviously of a metaphysical and paranormal nature, of course, but when faced with what appear to be inexplicable events, I constantly fight that as an all-too-easy trap.

Apparently, I was to learn, most people have the potential to send and receive telepathic messages, but only a tiny minority actually do so because most people never learn how to actually extend their "antennas" or turn on their "transmitters." So they can't receive or send, according to Paul. Whole new worlds of revelation and discovery open up to those lucky few who discover the secret. They are the masters—not unlike artistic geniuses—who, in turn, possess the ability to mentor others who seek to unlock the door to those hidden treasures of the mind.

But, as with most disciplines, the struggle to attain proficiency can be long and arduous, even assuming that one is fortunate enough to find a master willing to take on students. When one thinks of the likes of Beethoven, da Vinci, or Einstein, the thought of "teacher" does not spring to mind. We usually think of them as unique individuals blessed with special talents and abilities and recognize them for their accomplishments rather than as tutors.

But somehow, somewhere, for some reason, I apparently acquired at least a rudimentary ability to receive certain raw telepathic messages. Perhaps it was bestowed upon me for a specific purpose—initially to enable me to rendezvous with Paul, back in 1999.

Again, I must emphasize, this is according to Paul. As for me, I could just as easily accept it, reject it, or take a stance of neutrality.

At the time, his statement led me to a new belief that I was going to be given the opportunity to develop the skills that would allow me to ascend to the highest level of telepathic proficiency. That is, rather than merely receiving indefinite "hunches," I would someday be able to receive psychic communications as clearly and precisely as any voice message received over a telephone.[1]

Whether I would also develop a similar ability to transmit my thoughts to others just as clearly and precisely was not answered during this session. I do know that I had previously experimented with trying to transmit my thoughts to specific individuals, but never got any substantive confirmation that the messages were received.

---

[1] A bit of clarification is required here, particularly for those who have read my last book. I had discussed telepathy previously, had suspected on at least one occasion that I had received telepathic signals, and had been told by Paul during our initial meeting on that Easter Sunday in 1999 that I had been summoned via that medium. But at no time did I ever believe with a fair degree of certainty that I was a telepath of even the lowest order, or that I had ever engaged in a two-way telepathic conversation.

Yet it's possible, relaxing my skepticism for a moment, that I did get a "wrong number" once, so to speak. That was in August of 1998. An editor of a New Age magazine, who was interviewing me after my first book had just been published, thought she detected a certain psychic potential in me and encouraged me to at least give telepathy a try before rejecting it out of hand. So, figuring I had nothing to lose except perhaps a bit of my own sense of level-headedness, I decided to follow her advice. But how to go about it? I'm sure there must be books on the subject, probably in the New Age section—certainly not in the science section. But what did I know? Considering all that had happened to me recently, perhaps I was living in the Dark Ages, metaphysically speaking.

I knew I was going to feel somewhat sheepish, but the time had come to really open my mind—hopefully not so wide as to allow my brain to fall out—and attempt something that was well outside the realm of my beliefs and experience. I would have been mortified at the time if any of my mainstream friends had known what I was about to embark upon.

Anyway, there wasn't time to do any reading on the subject. I would just have to experiment. I made myself comfortable on the bed, propped a couple of pillows under my head, closed my eyes and concentrated on relaxing. I conjured up a mental image of the individual I wanted to contact, a female whom I had befriended a year earlier. (It was now August of 1998.) I had good reason to believe that she had the required abilities, if anyone did.

"Gina, it's Phil. Please contact me. Gina, it's Phil. Please contact me." I tried to project my thoughts by simply concentrating on directing them to the mental image of Gina that I held in my mind. I repeated the phrase silently several hundred times over a period of an hour or so.

Nothing. Finally I gave up and busied myself with some chores. I was right. I did feel foolish and silly.

However, I put aside some time and attempted it again the next day. This time, I went into the den, closed the shutters, turned out the light, and sat in the dark, staring into the colorful patterns of the ion storm of the *Star Trek* screen saver image. I let myself become mesmerized by the flowing lights, feeling that I was in a nearly trancelike state. Again I thought of Gina, and I silently repeated the same mantra.

The colorful, swirling patterns on the screen drew me in, and I became lost in time. I was not aware of my surroundings, only the hypnotic, psychedelic powers of the screen that seemed to envelop me. After what seemed like ten or fifteen minutes, I glanced up at the clock on the wall and was amazed to realize that two hours had passed.

All that time, I had continuously kept up the silent mantra.

Again, there was no response—not that I really expected any. This was just a playful exercise in what I considered metaphysical amusement, but I was alone in the house, I had time to kill, and I didn't see any harm in it. I actually approached it like a game, more entertainment than serious research. All the while, the logical part of my brain would surface periodically and sneer at me, asking me just what in blazes I was trying to prove. I ignored it.

Okay, I was satisfied. Mental telepathy either doesn't work or I lacked the powers or the knowledge to access it. I gave up, at least for the time being.

But things can look different in the light of a new day, especially after a good night's sleep, and the idea continued to intrigue me. So, having nothing better to keep my mind occupied the next day as I cleaned the kitchen, vacuumed the carpets, made the bed, and ran over to the post office to check the PO box, I played with a hundred mental variations on the theme during the day. I concentrated with furrowed brow; I mentally relaxed and tried to project gentle thoughts while thinking of Gina; I spoke the words out loud at times; I tried to visualize my thoughts as a physical beam that I projected outward. And so it went for most of the day.

No response, as far as I was aware.

And then an interesting thing happened.

Tired of being cooped up in the house, I grabbed a book and headed for the local mall, where I bought a diet soft drink and sat myself down at a table in the food court. The place was crowded with the usual teenagers just hanging out and probably trying to fill their boring summer day with some distraction, which typically takes the form of fertility-rite socializing.

I half-heartedly read a few paragraphs of the book I had grabbed, but my mind was wandering and I began thinking about my efforts to contact Gina. The din of the place receded into the background, and soon my brain had blocked out all distractions. I found myself totally focused on her. I was doing it again, almost subconsciously.

I spent minutes staring at the book and absentmindedly sipping my drink, becoming almost oblivious to my surroundings as my mind became totally preoccupied with trying yet again to send a telepathic message.

Finally, I became aware that an Asian teenage girl, very slightly built, who was sitting with three other girls at a table to my right, was speaking to me. She had said "excuse me" several times before I came out of my fog and it dawned on me that she was speaking to me.

"I'm sorry," I said, shaking my head to clear it, "I was lost in my book." It was a little white lie, but it was an easier explanation than trying to tell her that I was trying to commune with someone who wasn't there.

"Did you say something to me?" she asked.

She had penetrating brown eyes, which sparkled with curiosity, and she gave me an inquisitive smile.

"What? No, I . . . wait, weren't you speaking to me?" I asked awkwardly, feeling as though I had just stumbled and fallen on my behind in front of the whole food court. She obviously sensed my uneasiness. As pubescent girls are hormonally inclined to do at almost any time, she began giggling and was quickly joined by her friends.

"I thought you had spoken to me," I said.

"No, before that," she said. "Did you say something to me before I spoke to you?" Her friends began giggling even more.

We weren't getting anywhere so I excused myself and went back to my book and took another sip of my drink. This time I actually read a page or two. Three or four minutes passed and I considered strolling through the mall before heading back to the house. But before I could rise from my chair, the teenage girl got up and began walking toward the hamburger joint.

"Ginny, bring me some ketchup," one of her friends called after her, waving a single French fry. Ginny—or perhaps it was Jeannie or Jenny or something very similar—waved awareness of the request in return.

I was riveted to my chair. I smiled in sheer delight and amazement. *No way*, I thought. *This is just a coincidence.*

But was it *really* coincidence? Was it possible that the young girl—whose almond eyes and slight body build were not all that dissimilar to Gina's—had an ability, perhaps unrealized, to receive telepathic messages? And then there were the similar names, Gina and Ginny, or what sounded like Ginny. For one foolish moment, I considered trying to strike up a conversation with the girl so that I might stay in touch with her to possibly try some telepathic experiments later.

Suppose she really was a receiver for such messages? What a terrible, wasted opportunity if I let her just disappear from my life. Maybe she even had the ability—again, most likely unrealized—to also transmit extrasensory messages that others might be able to receive.

The young lady returned to her table and resumed the girlish, giggling interplay with her companions. On two occasions, I turned with the intention of talking to her, but backed down both times. I had to be realistic. I would have had to ask her name, and at least a phone number, if not her home address, if I were to befriend her and persuade her to take part in the test that I had in mind.

But common sense prevailed and I resisted the temptation. I thought of what my reaction as a parent would be if some old man had approached my daughter in such a fashion. So I took a final sip of my soda, got up, and went home.

Observation By Paul

"Try something. There is no glory in surrendering before you even know what challenge you face."

our paths cross

Months passed without significant incident after the encounter at the mall. Then on April 2, 1999, Good Friday, I was lying in bed about 6:30 a.m., fully awake but not yet ready to get up. I wasn't thinking of anything in particular as I luxuriated in the comfort of the warm bed, when I was suddenly overcome by a strange sensation that I found delightful and borderline sensuous. Next came a sense of mental clarity washing over me, sweeping away any lingering cobwebs of sleep. I knew I was lying in bed in my physical body, yet I felt that I somehow existed concurrently on another plane, in a remarkable dimension. It was a place that I knew, with all of my being, I had never visited before, and yet—strangely enough—a region in which I felt completely at home, as though I truly belonged there. The feeling was not unlike that of deja vu, although much more intense. My mind was crystal clear and in that clarity I understood that I was at the moment residing in a part of the brain that

I had never before consciously explored. How I had gotten there was a complete mystery.

Some people contend that we humans use only ten to fifteen percent of our brain capacity, the remainder lying fallow throughout our lifetimes. Then there are others who claim that is strictly a myth. Perhaps the truth lies somewhere in between: We all have the potential, which may someday be realized, to perform the various feats that certain adepts do with such facility. Somehow, I felt that I had crossed over into such an ethereal region—or had been pulled over by some unknown force. Whatever it was, I was there and I was enraptured.

And then it happened. I didn't hear the words spoken. I don't believe that I even cognitively thought them independently. The thought was just suddenly there in my mind.

Seek out the angel and you will be sought in return.

Then the door seemed to close and I returned to Earth, metaphorically speaking, back to that rather uninteresting, tedious part of the brain that carries most of us through our lives. The experience had occurred abruptly and was over quickly, but even so, I was convinced that I had momentarily been in some personally uncharted waters.

I knew instinctively, perhaps even intellectually—certainly emotionally—that this experience was profound. This was not just a random, meaningless thought that had popped into my head for no apparent reason. I was mystified by its meaning, by its significance, if any, and by its origin.

Seek out the angel and you will be sought in return.

What in the world could that mean? I thought, as I lay in bed for another hour pondering the experience. I even consciously sought to return to that wondrous dimension of lucidity, certain that I could find the answer there. But I was locked out, still residing in that side of the brain that yields no easy answers; I was banging on the portal to the other portion, to no avail.

Seek out the angel. Los Angeles is known as the City of Angels. Could that have something to do with it? Was I supposed to go to Los Angeles? That didn't seem to make much sense. I practically live in Los Angeles—just outside the city limits, but within Los Angeles County. Maybe I wasn't supposed to go anywhere but, rather, look inward—introspection is a form of seeking and can be done without moving a muscle. Then again, I had to give some consideration to the possibility that perhaps this was just my imagination working overtime.

Once again, I immediately rejected that notion; the experience had been too intense. I was firmly convinced that something strange was going on, but its obscurity was maddening.

About midafternoon, after my wife had left for work, I began straightening out the bookcase in the den when I came across my appointment calendar for 1998—or perhaps I was drawn to it. I don't even know why I had held onto it. As I curiously flipped through the pages, the entry for Sunday, April 26, 1998, caught my eye.

A light went on in my head and suddenly I understood. On that weekend in 1998 my wife and I had driven to San Francisco to attend a presentation by a noted author on angels, Doreen Virtue, with whom I had exchanged e-mail messages. I had never met her personally, but something about her, her books, and her messages intrigued me enough that I was willing to make the 700-mile round-trip drive to attend her lecture.

At one point during her presentation, she asked the audience if anyone could see the guardian angel that she said accompanied her at all times. A smattering of people raised their hands. I was not one of them.

However, some hours later, in the middle of the vast emptiness of the San Joaquin Valley in Central California as we hurtled homeward down the slice of asphalt and concrete known as Interstate 5, I casually turned to my wife and asked, "Did you see it?"

"What?" she asked, turning to look out of the side window.

"No, not out there. The angel," I said. "Did you see the angel that the writer was talking about?"

"I'm afraid not," my wife responded.

"Me, neither," I said, and we drove in silence for most of the remainder of the trip back home.

But I *had* seen it. It was standing behind her, towering at least a foot over her, perhaps six feet six inches to seven feet tall, an ethereal form in human shape that was paradoxically visible and yet transparent—an apparition. When I first became aware of her angel, I stared transfixed and my breathing became shallow. No gasps of surprise came from the audience, which puzzled me and caused me to consider several possibilities: Others were more receptive to the sighting of an apparition and thus would not express overt wonder; or perhaps I was hallucinating, had gone into some sort of hypnotic trance, and only I was seeing it. I had looked at my wife for some sign of confirmation, but saw none.

I really didn't want this to be happening; it was too uncanny for me. It seemed as though I had been lurching drunkenly through life for the previous year, and just when it seemed that I was getting my bearings again, some other extraordinary event would come along and flummox me.

Well, I was going to sit on this little incident. It would

remain my secret, at least until I got some answers, until I understood whether these things were bona fide or if perhaps I was starting to lose my marbles.

I stared at the figure behind the author, making an effort to study the eyes, the nose, the mouth, the shape of the face, but the more I stared the more I realized that I couldn't really focus on any part of the figure. I was getting an impression rather than a sharp picture. I soon discovered that if I looked slightly off center of the specter, using my peripheral vision, I actually got a much clearer view of it.

After her lecture, the author made her way downstairs to a table where she autographed copies of her books. The apparition stayed right with her!

I was drenched in sweat by the time my wife and I got out of the building, and I knew that my sticky shirt and wet forehead were due to more than just the heat of the day. I was emotionally rent.

Seek out the angel and you will be sought in return.

I would be told later that when the thought flashed through my mind on that Good Friday as I lay in bed, I had received a low-level telepathic message—a simple summons in the form of a compelling hunch that led me to the San Francisco Bay area where Paul approached me in a park and struck up a conversation.

As I have recounted elsewhere, we spoke for several hours. If I had to take a wild guess about his vocation, I would have speculated that he was either a man of the cloth or perhaps a religious scholar. However, he never gave me any indication that he was my guardian angel. That stunning bit of news would be revealed to me only after my second meeting with him, nine months later.

As he bid me adieu at the end of the day and began walking out of the park, I took off my glasses and rubbed a palm across my closed eyes, massaging my temples, as well. I don't see much without my specs. The world turns into a fuzzy, unfocused kaleidoscope of shapes, forms and smears of colors. I don't even have depth perception, and have never experienced that phenomenon because I have a medical condition known as strabismus in which both eyes don't work together to form a stereoscopic image. I have had this condition for a lifetime.

But suddenly, as I watched Paul walk away, the scene in front of me morphed into sharp focus. I was experiencing depth perception for the first time, in all of its breathtaking glory! The image was nothing short of miraculous. Looking out upon this simple earthly landscape—seeing the image as three-dimensional, in which objects projected themselves into space so that I could judge size, thickness, form, and distance—was mesmerizing. My world normally passes before me as a flat field, much the way one sees life on a movie screen, So to see the images jump out of that screen was more breathtaking than I could ever have imagined.

And then, just as suddenly, my vision returned to normal—blurry, flat, unfocused—and I replaced my specs. Mysteriously, Paul had disappeared from sight between the time my vision blurred again and then refocused with the aid of the lenses. I *should* have been able to see him because he still had some way to go before the path took him out of view. I was befuddled and enthralled, simultaneously. The 3-D image was a delight to behold, even if I had imagined it, and I was grateful for the experience. But was it authentic or just another tic from my mind's eye?

Hypnotism? A neat trick if it could be pulled off, which I doubted, particularly from a distance. And I'm certain that

I can't be hypnotized—short of being slipped a Mickey Finn or a dose of peyote.

I knew what I was doing: looking for a logical explanation for the seemingly inexplicable. If I found it, it would put my mind at ease, reaffirming my belief system. At the same time, a hidden part of me was mentally giving myself a swift kick in the pants for denying what would appear to be the obvious.

This was nothing short of a miracle.

It was Easter Sunday and I—a longtime atheist—had literally seen the light. I can't say that I "got religion." It was more like an awakening of some sort, an awareness of elements that are not normally part of my life. I wasn't resurrected, but I was convinced that I had been profoundly touched, by . . . something.

Observation By Paul

"If you want to witness a miracle, you have already done so. Just thinking the thought is a miracle, as is every moment that you exist."

a paradox
of terms

Let us flip forward again to 2001, to another miraculous encounter with Paul.

Here we were—an atheist and a guardian angel—sitting around a flaming fire pit at night in my gazebo. I had already come to terms with the fact that I could see angelic apparitions, if that was indeed what they were. I was also reconciled to the fact that there was an entity of some sort watching over me, and that his name was Paul. He clearly was a physical presence, which I would later learn is a rare occurrence under ordinary circumstances; when they appear at all for those few privileged individuals who have actually met their guardian angels, it is usually in an ethereal mode, as an apparition—as I had first observed in San Francisco in 1998.

I accepted his reality and yet I still referred to myself as an atheist, a seeming paradox if ever there was one! It was obvious to me that a drastic questioning of my belief system was in order, but whenever the thought arose, I always seemed to find a reason to defer acting on that compelling issue.

Even now, I still am not psychologically and emotionally prepared to deal with the problem, so I will continue, for the time being, to avoid what is bound to become a wrenching ordeal.

"So, I do have the ability to receive telepathic messages, then?" I asked Paul.

"Rudimentary ones on occasion, yes," he replied. "But, as I said, you have a long way to go before you will be able to achieve the level of proficiency needed to communicate fluently with other telepaths over great distances."

I was actually getting excited. *Telepathy.* Imagine that! The idea was nothing short of magical, especially for someone like myself, who had never considered such things possible. The idea that I might someday possess that power was intoxicating.

"Are you going to teach me?" I asked.

"You'll be given the opportunity to develop the innate abilities that most people possess but that few ever discover and utilize."

"Is that answer a yes or a no?" I asked with just a bit of exasperation.

Paul gave me a sidelong look of amused sufferance.

"A little testy, are we?" he asked with a sardonic smile.

"Sorry," I replied.

I still had work to do on developing certain social skills, such as showing patience. Paul really is a sweet and charming guy—in fact, angelic. I knew that I shouldn't be blaming him for my own shortcomings—specifically, my inability to not sweat the small stuff, or to accept people as they are without being critical.

"To answer your question, I'll undoubtedly have a hand

in it, but others will also be involved. The one who will be most responsible, though, is you. You will be required to do the work. No one else can do that for you," Paul said.

I stared at the dancing flames and noticed that the lava rocks in the fire pit were beginning to glow. I always enjoyed that.

Paul and I sat peacefully and silently for several minutes. I was lost in thought while he peered out into the darkness. Hundreds of individual lights sparkled across the valley that lay before us, and the effect can be hypnotic.

Finally, I shook myself from my reverie and asked Paul the purpose of his visit, why he had summoned me. I was glad to see him, of course, I assured him, but I was also curious about why he had chosen this time and this place to contact me again. After all, I hadn't seen him in nearly two years and, in fact, had not even been certain that I ever would meet up with him again.

"You called me," he said simply, "and I came."

I studied his face in the light of the dancing flames, looking for some indication that he was pulling my leg, but he appeared deadly serious.

I chuckled self-consciously, quite convinced that he had misspoken, so I pressed for clarification even as I tried to correct his misperception.

I called him? He had to be kidding. I was inside my house reading when I felt an inclination to follow a "hunch." And Paul had already admitted that he had transmitted the message toward me. I failed to see how that could be interpreted as a call from me to him. I was anxious to hear his explanation.

"How did you get here?" I asked as I walked across the lawn, opened the sliding glass door to the kitchen, and reached for my pack of cigarettes on the counter just inside.

"Why do you ask?" he replied as I returned to the gazebo and lit up a smoke.

"I was just thinking that maybe you rode in on a time warp, or whatever it is that gets you around, and that you're still stuck in it," I said playfully.

"What are you talking about? Wait, let me guess—you've taken up a foreign language. I'm sorry to burst your balloon, but speaking nonsense doesn't qualify."

Good old Paul. He can give as well as he gets. I laughed.

"Seriously, though, I understand what you are saying. But let me assure you that I am here because you called me."

I started to form a rebuttal, but he continued without pause, talking over my aborted response.

"Maybe *called* is the wrong word," he said. "Actually, you have been radiating vibes for help for several weeks now and it was that inner plea to which I responded."

I settled back into the seat in the gazebo, blew a plume of tobacco smoke into the darkness of the night, and resigned myself to giving my full attention to his explanation.

He said that I had been sliding headlong into a deeper and deeper funk with each passing day since September 11, although I had been refusing to acknowledge it. Millions of Americans, of course, had been involved in a terrible psychological struggle after that tragic day, and I considered that my feelings were pretty typical of what the average citizen was going through. Surveys had shown a quantum leap in the number of people who were suffering bouts of sleep difficulties. The sales of tranquilizers, antidepressants, sleeping pills, and alcohol had all risen dramatically. It was the natural and easily predictable result of the stress that Americans were experiencing as a direct consequence of a devastating event.

And, as I related in my last book, I and thousands of others were also dealing with a related event of almost unimaginable proportions. Although it did not involve the tragic loss of life and crushing economic havoc that were inflicted by the terrorist attacks, the incident was nevertheless a deep and bitter disappointment that compounded and intensified the feelings of loss that we shared with other Americans.[2]

"You're in trouble," Paul said. "You may not think so, but you are. You are disheartened and morose to the point where it is beginning to suppress your immune system. Depression can do that, you know. Were you aware of that?"

I flicked the cigarette butt into the flames and immediately lit up another. I nodded and replied that I had heard or read about that little bit of medical/psychological theory—or factoid, I suppose, if it is accurate.

"Worry, stress, anxiety—these can all suppress the immune system. And a suppressed immune system leaves a person vulnerable to attack from all kinds of diseases. I think that's pretty common knowledge," Paul continued.

I told him that I appreciated his concern for me but that it wasn't necessary, and assured him that I was fine. I will admit, though, that I had been feeling somewhat melancholy for weeks. And I seemed to be tired more than usual. I was spending a lot of time in bed, suffering headaches, feeling listless. I had lost interest in many of the everyday activities that kept me busy, and some of which actually used to bring me pleasure. These included the weekly mowing of the lawn, my daily walk/jog, doing the grocery shopping, puttering in the garage, and a host of other chores and pastimes. While not all of them typically brought me the same satisfaction as

---

[2] I choose for sound and specific reasons not to dwell upon that corollary event here, but for a fuller explanation I refer readers to my publisher's web site, originpress.com/krapf, where they can find free links to early chapters in my last book that will be helpful, and also to the Postcript of this book which gives an update on what I call the "Contact Project."

my newspaper and my books, I still had tackled them without hesitation before the funk had set in.

But I figured that my sluggishness was just a symptom of the perilous and challenging times that we were living in.

"And that's what I meant when I said that you sent for me," Paul said. "Not consciously, of course. But you were sending out fairly obvious grief signals indicating that you were walking a thin line and needed help. You wouldn't admit it, naturally; you cling to this anachronistic and mythical notion that it's unmanly to show feelings that you erroneously interpret as signs of weakness. And so you keep it bottled up inside, as millions of other men do, until it makes you sick or until it becomes too painful to bear and then you do something foolishly stupid and irreversible."

I leaned forward, rested my forearms on my thighs and stared into the fire. I took a deep drag on my cigarette and blew the smoke out in a stream that glistened white in the light of the flames and then disappeared in a swirl into the darkness.

"Maybe I was broadcasting distress signals, but to no one in particular," I mumbled, acknowledging for the first time, not only to Paul but to myself as well, that there had been times in the past month when I felt so heartsick that I really had to struggle with the daily demands of life.

"The message was getting louder by the day and I finally decided that I had to answer it, to intervene. You're feeling lost—and you don't know where to turn."

Several long moments of silence ensued.

"Look at me!" Paul said so abruptly that I flinched as his voice cut through the cool night air. My head snapped up and our eyes locked.

"What were you thinking right before I arrived?" he asked gently.

It seemed at the time to be a rather strange question. But I considered it and tried to recollect if I was doing or thinking anything of significance right before I got the urge to go roaming. After cogitating for several long moments, I couldn't think of anything that was particularly special or out of the ordinary. I simply had been reading a book about Otis Chandler, the former publisher of the *Los Angeles Times*, where I had spent most of my career. This book provided an account of the historic events leading up to the sale of the parent corporation to the Tribune Company of Chicago.

At least I had been trying to read, because I did recollect that my thoughts had been straying and I was having a bit of a problem concentrating. Then it came to me. I had been daydreaming, fantasizing, in those minutes before I reacted to my "hunch." Even as I thought about the entertaining little flight of imagination, it brought a smile to my face.

The licking blaze performed a rhythmic dance within the gazebo, spawning a show of flashing shadow and orange light, enough for Paul to see my cheerful expression.

Paul's expression, however, in contrast to mine, was not one of amusement; he was almost scowling, which puzzled me somewhat. I wondered why an innocent little smile on my part at this juncture would cause such a strained reaction.

As it turned out, it was a complete misunderstanding. He thought he knew what had come to my mind—a quite serious and disturbing memory—and he was concerned that I was taking it so lightly. In fact, he was wrong; at least I believed he was.

"It really is no laughing matter," he said.

"I'm not laughing, I'm just as mad as you are," I said with mock gravity, still smiling and barely suppressing a laugh.

"Okay, it's nothing to smile about then," he said.

I realized then how dead serious he was and so I quit the clowning around. I didn't know what he thought was on my mind when I was up in my room reading, but it certainly was nothing of any import, especially anything that would provoke such a reaction from him. The fantasy that I had found so entertaining actually involved finding myself on another planet populated by beings who were thousands and thousands of years more advanced than humans.

Or perhaps it was the Earth as I would visualize it thousands of years into the future—it wasn't really that specific. One thing is certain, though: It was a mental escape hatch from the here and now of Earth that opened onto a wonderful future world that offered not only peace, happiness, comfort, and contentment, but also excitement and personal fulfillment. It was a blissful world free of the travails that plague humanity, the odious events that are hammered relentlessly into our brains day after dismal day, year after year, by newspapers and TV and radio—and now also by the Internet. It seems to me that—little by little, like an eternal river grinding away at the landscape—this unrelenting and virtually inescapable assault must have some effect upon the sensibilities. I believe it has the ability, at least in some, to erode the spirit, chip away at optimism, and drown enthusiasm in a swiftly flowing current of despair, until finally the senses become dulled. Some pessimists may even lose all hope that the human condition will ever improve.

How does one seek respite from the onslaught? Well, there are any number of methods that have the effect of dulling the senses: alcohol; prescription pain-killers, tranquilizers, or other medications; the street drugs, like rock cocaine, or heroin. Still others may seek refuge by pulling the comforting cloak of religion snugly over their heads. Others, such as myself, simply free our minds and soar off into the cosmos on the wings of our own imaginations. We leave the present

Earth trillions upon trillions of miles or thousands of years behind as we create for ourselves a new domain where God's in his heaven—metaphorically speaking in my case, of course—and all's right with the world, to paraphrase the poet Robert Browning.

"It was nothing," I said reassuringly. "Just a simple escapist fantasy. Why?"

"You weren't thinking of suicide?" he asked solemnly.

The question caught me completely off guard.

"What? Of course not! That's absurd!"

But it wasn't, really.

There was no doubt that I had been struggling with bouts of the blues—some may choose to call it depression—and the thoughts of suicide *had* popped into my head periodically. But I know as surely as I know up from down that I never once seriously considered acting upon those thoughts. Thoughts of suicide are a natural and typical symptom of depression, but in most cases that's all they are—thoughts. Most depressed people don't act upon them.

As it turned out, Paul and I simply differed in our interpretations of how I was responding to these feelings of discouragement and demoralization. I saw my little flights of fancy in which I spent more and more time imagining myself living in another time or another place as simple daydreaming. I'll even admit that I was engaged in a form of escapism, which I considered harmless. These imaginary wanderings took me light-years into the cosmos or to a distant future Earth in which humans had evolved into highly advanced creatures who no longer had to *hit* one another to make a point.

But while I considered these mental meanderings innocuous, Paul saw in them something more ominous, and that is why he had come calling. The incidents had become more and more frequent, he said, and I was spending greater chunks of time engaged in this pastime.

But again, so what? I considered them harmless; he saw something sinister in them. I couldn't agree with him on that one, no matter how smart he was. You may say that angel perception trumps human perception, but this was borderline silliness, in my view. Still, I held my tongue.

I appreciated and respected Paul's concern for me, but I believed that he was misinterpreting and overreacting. I was of the opinion that eventually I would shake off these blues and everything would again be fine. Nevertheless, he insisted that I needed him to be available to me for a while. Being my guardian angel, he had the option of being with me constantly, I suppose. But he wanted more than that.

"I think we should meet on a regular basis for a few months and just talk," he said.

"Like a shrink?" I asked, teasingly.

"Something like that, but at a much cheaper hourly rate," Paul retorted.

"I'm game," I said, "although I still insist that I'm fine and don't really need a shrink. I'll just look upon our sessions as visits by a friend."

"There's a secondary reason. I want to guide you on a journey," he said. "There is some important work ahead for you and I need to help prepare you for it."

We agreed that Paul would visit me regularly, although there was no set schedule. Did that mean daily? Several days a week? Weekly? I would just have to wait and see. I was looking forward to it.

"Happy birthday," he said, then simply walked away and vanished into the night air.

I don't care if I live a million years. I still will never fail to be awed by such seemingly supernatural events. They are just downright spooky and eerie.

Upon viewing a present-day illusionist's stage show, anybody from a couple of centuries ago—no matter how refined and learned—would surely believe that they were witnessing magical or supernatural events. We modern-day spectators, of course, would be too sophisticated to believe it. We know it's a trick . . . don't we?

And then the flames in the fire pit went out.

Observation by Paul

"It is not a sign of weakness for a drowning person to call for help or to accept a helping hand."

angels aren't perfect

As I headed for the stairs to return to the bedroom, my wife, who was watching television in the living room, casually asked me what I had been doing. Our preferences in TV fare don't often mesh, so by unstated but mutual agreement she usually parked herself in the evenings on the sofa in front of the large-screen TV, while I propped myself up in bed to watch a set in the upstairs bedroom.

Her tastes run to sports programs, sitcoms, *Star Trek, The X-Files,* and romantic movies. I have little interest in sports, can't abide sitcoms, find the *X-Files* and *Star Trek* hopelessly unrealistic, and don't have the temperament to sit through mushy movies.

I told her that I had just been out getting a breath of fresh air and grabbing a smoke—an incongruous statement if ever there was one. But my wife, if she caught the irony of it, gave no indication and she went back to her program as I continued upstairs.

I didn't then know much about guardian angels, but from what little bit of religious dogma I was aware of, only the so-called God was omniscient, omnipotent, and omnipresent—and absolutely perfect. Angels might be divine and heavenly beings, but since they aren't God, they can't be perfect. And if they aren't perfect, they certainly are capable of being wrong and making mistakes. At least that's the way I looked at it.

I did not believe that I was truly suicidal, despite the occasional random thought along those lines, but nevertheless I looked forward to spending the time with Paul. He was a fascinating companion, and if he wanted to keep a close eye on me, that was fine with me—even if I disagreed with his motivation. It also seemed to me that he could quite easily have kept an eye on me even while staying out of sight. I figured that face-to-face meetings would be required for therapy sessions, however.

I thought back to our conversation and ran it over and over in my mind. He didn't want to meet just to monitor me. There was a dual purpose. He also wanted to guide me on a journey because there was some important work ahead for me. He said he wanted—no, he said he needed—to help prepare me for it. I was somewhat puzzled by that, but it was nevertheless intriguing and exciting. I was receptive to the idea of a new adventure to spice up retirement life.

Back in my bedroom, I didn't feel like returning to the book on Otis Chandler at the moment, so I did a quick surf of the TV channels. Nothing grabbed me and I soon began entertaining myself with a daydream. It followed the typical story plot: living in a future time on Earth when humans had come to their senses and finally understood that the whole purpose of life—in my secular view, at least—is to enjoy it. And that's what I was doing, enjoying it, until I finally dozed off and had to face the real night-time dream world, the one where I surrendered editorial control over the story and let my subconscious take over.

By the weekend my previously mentioned surgery was sufficiently healed to allow me to resume my exercise regimen, so I headed for the trails that crisscross the hills, dales, glens, and meadows that surround my neighborhood housing development. It's actually possible to find oneself alone on portions of the trails back in the hills. Well, almost alone. Cottontails constantly hop across the path and dart into the chaparral; hawks circle lazily and silently overhead on thermals, scouring the hillsides for a meal; squirrels and gophers abound, as do a variety of chirping birds that populate the giant California oaks.

In this pastoral setting, with a warm sun bathing me from a clear blue sky, when I am alone with my thoughts, it is as close as I ever come to what I suppose might be termed a religious exercise. This is my church and I attend it regularly.

Why was I not surprised when the man who appeared in the distance coming around a turn in the trail turned out to be Paul, decked out in a jogging outfit? If I remember correctly, the morning was a bit cool so the clothes were not altogether inappropriate for the weather, but there was something weird and comical, I thought, about an angel in such a get-up. This moment was a prelude of what was to come for many, many months. I wondered momentarily if the clothing was merely cosmetic for Paul or if it also served, as it did for me, as protection against the elements.

As the course of events was soon to reveal, Paul would show up unexpectedly at any time of the day under a wide variety of circumstances and locations, both public and private. He sometimes appeared in the evening as I read or watched television. On more than one occasion, my heart jumped into my throat when he unexpectedly appeared— literally materialized out of thin air—beside me as I was driving. I ran into him at the grocery store, at the local mall, at neighborhood parks. It seemed there was no getting away from him even if I wanted to, which I never did. He was, after all, my personal guardian angel.

But more often than not our meetings were pre-arranged and were conducted on a fairly regular basis of four or five times a week. Few of our get-togethers lasted less than an hour, and it wasn't unusual for them to stretch out for three or four hours. There were even several marathon sessions that took up the better part of a day. Most of our encounters took place in the open, often in public places.

Southern Californians revel in the outdoors, and I, for one, am convinced that there is no more perfect weather in the universe than the winter months here, especially during droughts when there isn't enough rain to raise a stink on a mule. After all, it is a desert, so most of the water we need for serving a burgeoning population is imported. Barely a trace of moisture had fallen in the Southland during the traditional rainy season of November through March for the previous two years, and on this November day in 2001 there did not appear to be any end in sight for this protracted dry period. Of course, those gorgeous days often come at a price—when man or nature sets the hills ablaze.

By this time of year in the Southland, the heat of summer has typically dissipated, the inversion layer that traps the smog has lifted and allows the sky to sparkle a brilliant aquamarine blue, and most of the tourists have gone home, thinning the traffic on the freeways and the crowds at local attractions, providing residents like Paul and me a bit more breathing room.

During the next seven months I took several airplane flights and Paul was on each of them, although he never occupied a seat. I suppose that meant he wasn't a ticketed passenger. I would look up and there he would be, walking the aisle! In each case he appeared to me as just one of many passengers. The first time it occurred, I was more than surprised—I was amazed. What was his purpose? Certainly he could have met me at my destination and didn't need to be on the plane.

I'm pretty sure that angels can get around quite nicely without relying upon man-made contraptions of transport. It soon became obvious that his purpose was to be at my side—to let me know he was there—rather than merely hitching a ride. Even though he appeared in seemingly physical form, appropriately attired, it was pretty obvious that he was visible only to me. He never spoke to me on the flights, a dead giveaway that others couldn't see him and a not-so-subtle indication that I was not to speak to him. He did acknowledge me with a smile and slight nod as he passed my seat on his way to wherever he might be heading in the celestial realms.

In January of 2002, I saw him on a flight to Kansas City, Missouri, and he was there also on the return flight. He was also with me in March of the same year when I flew to Seattle, where a strange thing happened. I was to give a talk at the Ramtha School of Enlightenment outside of Seattle in the town of Yelm, Washington.

That evening, as I began to address the audience of several hundred people, I suddenly froze. The words wouldn't come out. My mind went blank. As I stared at my notes, fishing for something to say, I became uncomfortably aware of the hundreds of faces gazing up at me. For the first time since I had started speaking to audiences large and small, I was on the verge of panicking.

As I said, this was very strange, given that I had long before conquered my fear of public speaking. I had gone from being someone who dreaded the very thought of it to someone who never feared an audience again. In connection with tours in support of my first two books, I had addressed literally millions of people on radio, TV, and in personal appearances, and had never given it a second thought. The issue was quite simple: These were mere human beings that I was addressing. No matter how lofty their positions, whether they were kings or presidents, captains of industry or generals of the military, celebrated movie stars or anonymous members of the audience who sat in darkened theaters watching the stars, they all had one thing in common—they were mere mortals, just like myself. I had recently come to accept the certainty that the universe was populated with intelligent life forms, a radical departure from my previously held belief that regarded this as a preposterous idea. But it finally occurred to me that the cosmos was simply too big not to contain other life; such an idea was as ludicrous as believing that Earth's oceans contained only one species of fish. The law of averages would dictate also that many of those extraterrestrial creatures would be far more technologically advanced than humans. Ergo, compared to the magnificent extraterrestrial creatures that surely must populate the vast cosmos, human beings would be considered quite unspectacular and certainly not capable of inspiring the same sense of reverence and wonder. I just knew that "out there" were some glorious, magnificent, noble, intelligent creatures—and I had met some. In that context, how could I ever again be intimidated by any mere human, who would be quite ordinary and plebeian by comparison?

And then there was one other little detail that also played a part in my transformation. Unknown to me at the time, Paul had—in the early days of my speaking career—laid a calming hand upon the fluttering butterflies in my stomach, or so he said.

Yet here I was, standing before the Ramtha group, finding myself uncharacteristically tongue-tied, struggling to say something—anything—to break the awkward silence.

After a few bungling attempts, during which time the audience sat in complete silence, I was able to choke out a couple of sentences that finally opened up the train of thought from which began flowing the words that would carry me through my presentation.

And the reason for my sudden bout of discomfiture? Just as I had begun to make my opening remarks, my eyes fell upon Paul standing smack in the middle of the seated crowd, his arms folded across his chest and a slight smile playing across his face. It was the first time I had ever seen him at any of my talks, and it rattled me. I don't know why; I should have expected it, I suppose. Nevertheless, I attributed my bumbling start to him—my mind being stuck on what his presence may have signified—rather than on my presentation.

Had he made himself visible to the others? Was he actually a member of the Ramtha group and known by others in the crowd—not as an angel, of course, but as just a regular guy?

This must have been Paul's mischievous nature coming into play. He does have a definite personality, a liveliness that can be fun much of the time, but that also can unnerve.

After I looked up a second time while struggling to emit even a sputter to break the silence, feeling for one of the few times in my life that I might actually swoon, Paul was nowhere to be seen. And then the motor kicked over, began to hum, and the words came pouring out. I was off and running, and the rest of the evening proceeded smoothly, with barely a hitch or pause for the next several hours.

If the audience or the sponsors were in any way put off by my less-than-loquacious start, there was no indication of it.

Later, in the bedroom at the compound where I was spending the night, Paul and I had a conversation. He had walked alongside me from the lecture hall to my room—a clear indication that his presence was unknown to others. I spoke in hushed tones so my voice wouldn't carry beyond the bedroom door. After all, if others in the household were to hear a one-sided conversation going on in my room, they just might rightfully get spooked. Although I could hear Paul clearly, he assured me that no one else was able to. I took his word for it.

I was still miffed that he had nearly caused me to panic at the beginning of my presentation earlier, and I gave him a piece of my mind, a difficult thing to do in whispers. We talked for an hour before Paul said goodnight and vanished. I dozed off almost immediately.

Observation By Paul

"The universe contains wonders beyond imagination, but there is no such thing as a perfect mortal."

the nature of the job

The day Paul fell in beside me on the trails during my first walk after my surgery was only the first of many encounters we would have after that surprise visit to my gazebo. Shortly after he joined me we spotted a runner coming up the trail.

"When we pass that jogger coming toward us, will she see me talking to another person or just babbling to myself?" I asked.

He was smiling. I would eventually get to the point where I could intuitively determine when to carry on a public conversation with him, but initially I sought some kind of confirmation.

"It's okay to talk with me now. I'm in visible mode for all to see!" he said expansively. He threw out his arms and turned his movie-star face, eyes closed, to the sunny sky, obviously luxuriating in this setting in the great outdoors. I expected him, at any moment, to bellow to the heavens about what a glorious day it was and how good it was to be alive, or at least to exist. But how does one even begin to describe an angel's state of mind? Do angels have moods? He certainly seemed to be in an ebullient one, if so.

"She's not going to think you are nuts," he continued.

We exchanged "good morning" greetings with the woman as she jogged past us. She seemed to have an even brighter smile for Paul than she flashed at me. I can see how he would have that effect on the ladies. I have to admit that he is quite a handsome . . . angel.

My earlier concern was back: If we were going to be meeting on a regular basis, I had to have some operating guidelines. I needed to know how to distinguish when he was visible just to me—whether in seemingly physical form or as an apparition—from those times when others could see him as well. That way, at least I would know when it was politic to speak openly to him in front of others and when to remain silent.

Paul explained that he could materialize and dematerialize at will, and had the option to appear either as an apparition or in physical form. In the vast majority of cases, particularly as an apparition, he would be visible only to me. When he appeared in physical form, typically it was for my benefit only, although in certain infrequent circumstances he would also be detectable by others. He said he had complete control over all of those situations and conditions.

There was one other permutation: In physical form, his body could have mass or it could be "ethereal." When he had mass, others could detect him as easily as they can see, feel, or hear anyone else. That is, on a crowded sidewalk he would have to do his share of dodging, just as others do, lest he physically collide with someone.

However, when his physical appearance took ethereal form, which was by definition undetectable by others but completely visible to me, he could freely stroll an airplane without fear of such collision. The serving cart and the flight attendant—as well as passengers moving about—would pass right through him!

I've indicated that this was soon to occur on a number of occasions, and it is a sight for which mere words can do no justice.

I should emphasize that in the annals of all the world's religions—or so I am told—there are exceptions, times when seraphs, for one reason or another, wish to make themselves visible as apparitions to specific others. Let's face it, it most likely would frighten the devil—so to speak—out of the vast majority of people; they would think they had just seen a ghost. And materializations in physical form were even more rare in the historic record.

"I was talking to somebody who fancies himself quite knowledgeable on this subject, and he said that angels almost invariably appear as apparitions," I pointed out to Paul.

"That's quite right. It's not common for an angel to appear in a corporeal form," Paul responded.

"So, when I see you ... " I paused, groping for the right word to describe his presence. "Is that the proper term for it—*corporeal*? That's the word you just used. I was thinking of a simple term like *embodied* or *carnal*, or something like that."

"Yes, those would be accurate. Also *somatic*, I suppose," he said.

"Anyway, let me get this straight; when I see you in physical form it's possible that you are visible only to me, right?"

"Correct. Unless I have no reason to remain unseen by others, in which case I will appear to them as just another stranger. However, as I said, you will always know when that circumstance arises. Either I will inform you or you will be able to tell by my behavior."

"Okay, I think I'm starting to get it. And when you appear as an apparition, is that a sure sign that no one else can see you?"

Not only could they not see him when in the form of an apparition, he replied, but in most cases they could not detect him with any other sense, such as sound or touch.

Thus, under our informal agreement, his appearance as an apparition would simply serve to signify to me that only I could see him at the time. That way, I would instantly know it would be a good idea not to address him openly lest I appear to others to be "a strange man talking to himself." The incident at the lecture by the author in San Francisco came to mind.

"Why . . . I mean, what circumstances would oblige you to make your presence known to others in the form of a spirit? Besides the person you belong to? Wait, that didn't come out right. That sounds arrogant, as though I am claiming that you belong to me. Sorry, I wouldn't be so presumptuous. I meant the person you are visiting or talking with at the time. I don't know if I'm making myself clear," I said, annoyed with my clumsiness.

Paul chuckled. "Relax. I know exactly what you mean. There could be a multitude of good reasons, but let's take the lecturer as an example. Her spirit guardian stood behind her as an apparition, right? Well, she invited her audience to take a gander. You and a smattering of others saw the presence because it was cooperating with her."

"It was like a favor to her, then?"

"You could call it that."

"Why didn't everybody see it?" I asked.

"Why didn't you respond when she asked for a show of hands? You didn't, as you'll recall."

"I don't know, I guess I was a little embarrassed," I sputtered.

"Do you think some others might also have felt the same way?"

"Yeah, maybe. Probably. I understand what you're getting at," I said.

"I'm just saying that could be one of the reasons. Another one, also very likely, is that most of the people really *didn't* see it. You and a few others were the exception."

"How so? I mean, why?"

"A more developed natural ability," he said simply.

"Whoa, like a talent of some sort? Imagine that, me with a talent. Makes me feel kind of special," I said. But I think my effort to control my smirk didn't quite succeed.

Paul just gave me a dismissive sideways glance that told me I had just invited a biting riposte. Perhaps because I had said it in jest is why he let it slide and said nothing. The *look* had said it all.

I was breathing heavily as we reached the crest of a hill at the end of one leg of the trails that emptied out onto the main street circling the tract. We walked along the thoroughfare and came to another trail entrance to the hills, turning down into it.

"Not exactly accurate," he said.

He was back to his old habit of throwing out statements that required explanation, but which he didn't provide. Oftentimes I had to grill him to find out what page he was on; I was usually several pages behind.

"You're thinking only of recent times since you became aware of our relationship," he continued. "But you've seen me in the past, going back to your childhood."

He was being deliberately provocative. Two could play that game. After a few moments of silence, when he saw that I wasn't going to take the bait, he pressed on.

"But you never acknowledged me and I never introduced myself. You dismissed occasional brief glimpses of me as tricks of the eyes or of the light."

We were now headed down a steep incline on the trails. The trees and chaparral, as well of the hills themselves, were throwing shorter shadows. As the morning grew later, more walkers—with and without dogs—and joggers began to dot the landscape. I studied his countenance. He was truly enjoying himself, I assumed, based upon his beaming face. And the truth of matter is, I also was feeling fantastic. And why not? It was a lovely day.

"You thought you had seen a ghost," he said.

Oh. Ohhhh! It finally sunk in. Of course I had seen ghosts when I was a kid. What child hasn't? But as I aged, I determined that those sightings were nothing more than heightened childhood imagination. Like most kids, I loved scaring myself—and others as well—with tales of ghost sightings and other events designed to send a cold shiver of fear down the backbone. That's why we spent many a Saturday sitting through continuous showings of such delightfully frightening films as the comedians Abbot and Costello meeting up in spine-tingling action with *Wolfman, Dracula*, or *Frankenstein*.

"You're not telling me that some of the ghosts that I supposedly saw as a kid were real?" I asked.

"Apparitions," Paul replied.

"What?"

"Not ghosts. Apparitions. And, yes, some of those sightings could have been more than a mild hallucination, a trick of the light, a speck of dust in a watery eye, or any number of other misinterpretations."

I would guess that almost everyone at some time in life thinks he or she has seen a ghost. But those of us who don't believe in such things don't take the stories seriously. Still, there must be a reason why such tales have been told over the ages in every corner of the world.

Paul offered his own interpretation. For those who are convinced that they have sighted a phantom at one time or another, there's a possibility that they did see something that could be interpreted as supernatural. But it wasn't a ghost. It just very well may have been an angel in transparent form and it was no accident that they saw it. It is a reminder that angels are seen when they want to be, or at least when they are not concerned about being seen. It might have been the person's own spirit guardian, or someone else's. It is rare, but on occasion—according to Paul—one's angel, when appearing in transparent form, does allow itself to be seen by others for specific reasons and purposes.

"That's another thing," I said. "If angels almost always appear as apparitions, why do I see you so much in physical form?"

"I feel that it's important for me to appear in a personified form for the time being to give you a solid sense that you are talking to someone real—not a phantom, not a spirit, not a figment of your imagination. I want you to interact with me on the basis of man to man. I repeat: It's important."

It was at this point that Paul made it abundantly clear—although he had earlier touched upon the subject tangentially—that many of our sessions were essentially going to consist of talk therapy. Despite my contention that it wasn't necessary, he decided to take on the responsibility of personally counseling me, just to be sure that I got the treatment that he believed I needed.

I saw no point in arguing with an angel, so a regular regimen of sessions was scheduled. Actually, I liked them and I followed through on my vow to treat them as visits with a dear friend rather than as therapy with a doctor. In that respect, I also questioned him on his qualifications and wondered if he could be charged with practicing medicine without a license.

"What makes you think I'm unlicensed?" he asked dryly. Touché. He nailed me on that one.

As we strolled on, I remained rather intrigued by the visible/invisible business, the phantasmal versus the somatic presence, the tangible vis-à-vis the ethereal. It took much explaining, but I believe I finally got it sorted out. By the time he was through clarifying—during which time we must have walked a couple of miles, passing half a dozen or more people—a number of other pressing questions that I was dying to ask also had been answered.

Most people, of course, never see their guardian angels. However, a significant number become aware of them on a spiritual plane, somehow detecting the presence without actually seeing it. Those same people actually may see someone else's divine protector at some period in their lives. I am reminded of all the people who have seen Paul with me, never realizing that he was more than just another face in the crowd, far beyond what he appears to be.

On those occasions when the spirit/protector of a particular person does reveal its presence visually, it is, as I have noted, usually as an apparition. I can imagine a gentle, religious person waking during the middle of the night to behold a spirit in the darkness. This has never happened to me, but in my imaginary scenario the person is not afraid but actually quite welcoming to the visitor. And why not? This person is a believer whose faith is simply confirmed by the angelic presence. A soft, peaceful conversation between the two would not be surprising—maybe even expected.

For example, when I was a kid I heard my paternal grandmother talking to a relative about how she periodically awoke during the night to find an angel on her bed, stroking her silver locks. It gave me the willies at the time. I figured she was loco.

For those people who do become aware of their guardians—and the vast majority never do, according to Paul—the relationship typically begins with the distinct feeling of a presence of some sort that can range in perception from a vague sense of connection to an undeniable conviction of a spiritual linking.

Of course, I would have to classify myself as one of the lucky ones, being among those privileged individuals who not only have become aware of their divine guardian, but who actually see the angel in its many forms. I have now seen Paul both as an apparition—visible to me only—and as a somatic presence, seemingly wearing everyday street clothes—visible only to me at times but also to others at other times. And finally there is the completely incarnate appearance when his physical presence is as real to any one person as it is to all other people, capable of being seen, heard, and bumped into.

I personally know at least two people who "talk" with their personal angels on a regular basis but who have never seen the protector. Nevertheless, they are as certain of their presence and existence as they are of the bills that arrive on a regular basis in their mailboxes. And they are just as convinced that it is a two-way conversation, even if they never actually "hear" a response from the angel through their auditory system. The connection is spiritual, not physical.

I thought I was beginning to understand.

Observation By Paul

"Invisible things exist as surely
as empty space itself."

the big question

It was only a matter of time before I would ask Paul "the question." On one of those picture-perfect days, while Paul and I took simple pleasure in observing a group of mothers watching over their brood of preschoolers squealing in delight as they scampered around a play area at a neighborhood park late in the morning, I finally decided I would pose it.

I had already rehearsed the scenario in my mind: "Is there a God?" I would ask him quietly.

Yet I had also wondered why I even had to ask. The answer seemed axiomatic, even to me. If guardian angels existed, then it stood to reason that God did also. How could it be otherwise?

Paul's very being, which I fully accepted, was challenging one of my core beliefs—or non-beliefs. I could see Paul, talk with him, touch him; that required no leap of faith on my part. And I had actually seen him materialize and dematerialize before my eyes, which in itself would be enough to convince most people that they had witnessed a miracle of divine origin.

Yet, I was still not convinced. A natural explanation for Paul's superhuman powers could not yet be ruled out, and would be more to my satisfaction.

The ultimate question of God's existence was a different matter. Once I reached adulthood I had personally never believed in God, and my time spent with Paul would never be complete if I didn't pose the question, I had told myself on numerous occasions. I could no longer shunt the question aside, as I had been doing, pretending it wasn't there.

The setting was just right. This was the kind of day that tapped into the human capacity to appreciate the sublime beauty of nature that lay before us in soul-satisfying grandeur, and the innocent joy of young children was on display before us. But now that the moment had arrived, I found myself unable to get the words out. My mouth worked fruitlessly, moving in an effort to form the words, but bringing forth only silence. I managed to choke out a couple of grunts, a stammered word or two, but that was all. My futile efforts pulled Paul's attention off the group of mothers and their children and he eyed me curiously.

What in the world was going on? I was perplexed. In actual fact, it was as though I literally had been struck dumb. I took a deep breath, consciously made an effort to calm myself, to collect my wits. While I was baffled and confused by my vain efforts, I was at the same time fascinated by the psychological and emotional forces obviously at work. I waved off Paul's curious looks, gave him a reassuring smile, and spent several minutes in intense reflection.

And then I came to what I considered to be a reasonable conclusion. I couldn't force the words out because I knew that whatever answer Paul might give me, whether a definitive "yes" or "no" or a qualified alternative, I wouldn't accept it. That has nothing to do with my trust of Paul. In fact, it springs from everything that I had learned from him over the previous few months, to wit: No one can answer that question for another. The answer resides within each person, and only through a journey of introspection and discovery can the answer be revealed. For some, it is a short and easy jaunt. For others, the trail is tortuous, rugged and seemingly interminable. Some people make the pilgrimage for a lifetime and never see the end of the road. It is likely that I am one of those latter individuals.

I think most people's religious beliefs are absorbed by osmosis from their parents or other caregivers, or from the culture in which they are raised. I don't have any studies in front of me to back that up, just empirical evidence based upon my own interaction with people. I personally don't know anyone among my friends, relatives, or acquaintances who arrived at their beliefs by embarking upon a scholarly quest, comparing the various beliefs and philosophies, and then determining which one made the most sense to them. When it comes to religion, my gut instinct tells me that too many people don't want to educate their children, they want to indoctrinate them. And I believe that's just what happens in most cases.

I never adopted my parents' religious leanings, although I must admit that they never really tried to push their beliefs on me. My father tried halfheartedly to expose me to his church but I had too many questions that he couldn't answer to my satisfaction, so he gave up after a while. He thought I was a smart aleck.

My tendency to ask questions—or to at least harbor doubts when it was impolitic to voice them—goes pretty far back, at least to a tenth-grade English class during which we were discussing religion, of all things. Well, others were; I didn't get involved. A fellow student expressed a belief that God existed but that he doesn't—or isn't able to—exercise any authority over the lives of humans. I believe that's the philosophy known as *deism*. Immediately the teacher interrupted him with a supercilious objection equivalent to a tsk tsk. Oh, no, no, no, my goodness, no, was her reaction, and she then blessed us with *the truth*. God is the creator and the ruler of the universe who is very much involved in human affairs, she informed us. I believe that's somewhat of a theist philosophy. Now, I was never what one would call the scholarly type, but even I saw the giant hole in that kind of argument. Yet I also wasn't the kind of kid who challenged authority, at least not openly.

I remember the name of the teacher and the name of my classmate, who is now a retired professor from Stanford University and the author of a scholarly work on European cathedrals. Both the teacher and student were debating beliefs based upon faith, and faith is belief in something for which there is no evidence. Ergo, the student's belief was just as valid as the teacher's. However, I bit my tongue and kept that opinion to myself. I personally was not a believer in either position. It's possible that both were merely parroting what others had told them, who were told by others before them, who were told by others before them, ad infinitum all down the line to the very beginning.

It slays me when people talk like they have acquired a monopoly on universal truths, as if they singularly hold the key to the mysteries of creation. For some reason, although I haven't traveled widely, such talk conjures up in my mind an ignorant, semi-literate old man spouting his "wisdom" to a following of equally uneducated rustics living in wretched poverty in some backwater.

But this is Paul we are talking about, a guardian angel. Surely his word would be more authoritative, more credible than that of a mere mortal?

But how do I know that for sure?

I don't.

Paul didn't have to spell it out for me, but one of the lessons that I learned over the course of our meetings led me to the conclusion that he was not going to be providing me with a spiritual or religious education; he was not going to bestow upon me a quick study in theology. If I happen to gain some knowledge and wisdom through an inner journey that leads to illumination, then I should consider myself fortunate. However, even if I never find the answer, the pilgrimage itself is worth the effort because of all the interesting and revealing places it takes one. There is no success or failure in the search. There is only the journey.

I thought I understood. People who proclaim to believe— or disbelieve—in God because someone else said it is so have not found the answer. They haven't asked the question: *How in hell do **you** know?* They haven't asked for proof, for the evidence. They simply swallowed what they were fed.

But that's no answer. In court, that's called hearsay— repeating what someone else allegedly said—and is inadmissible as evidence.

And so the question, *Is there a God?*, is meaningless unless it is asked of oneself. The courtroom and the jury are within.

That is, paradoxically, the answer to the riddle. At least that's the way I see it.

I opened with a different question. "Are there times when you are not by my side?" I asked. "I mean, are you with me all the time?"

"From birth to death," he replied simply.

"Amazing," was all I could muster at the moment. I had become aware of him less than three years earlier, and yet he had been my constant companion for sixty-seven years, if his statement was accurate. I had no reason to believe that angels lie, so I accepted his word.

"All guardian angels?" I asked.

He gave me a questioning look.

"Are all guardian angels on duty 24/7 for a lifetime, or is that just your particular duty?"

"It's more than just a nine-to-five job," he said, giving me a knowing wink. "However, that is not to say that I cannot be elsewhere at times when it is in your best interests."

We moved on through the park. In a way, I was feeling cheated. I had wanted to ask a question that people had been asking since the first intelligent ancestors of humans started pondering the world around them. But whether or not there is a God, I had realized that Paul was not the one who would provide me the answer. Again, I was willing to admit that Paul's very existence, if I understood it correctly and wasn't being deceived, could make a strong argument for the affirmative.

And there were other questions, millions of them. I could imagine the inquiries early humans must have formulated as they surveyed the wonders of a world whose workings were, to their primitive knowledge, nothing short of magical and miraculous. How do the sun, moon and stars stay up in the sky without falling? Why does the moon change shape? What causes the ground to shudder like a wild animal and burst forth in fiery anger? Where do the wind and rain come from? What causes the heavens to flash with streaks of fiery light and to roar and rumble with such fury as to strike sheer terror into the hearts of the bravest of men and women? What is the source of the water that falls from the sky?

Science, of course, has provided the answers to all of those early fundamental questions. But so many questions remain unanswered, and I was frustrated that the best hope I had to find the solutions—in the form of Paul—was not about to hand them to me, as I had once thought he could. The search must be continued.

"I have a serious privacy concern," I told Paul.

"How so?" he asked.

"Well, if you are always at my side, and have always been at my side, does that mean that nothing I do ever escapes your notice? There are stalls around toilets in public restrooms for a reason. A man and a woman together—I mean, some things just require privacy."

"I'm your *guardian* angel. The stress is on *guardian*," he said. "I watch over you. I try to keep you out of harm's way. I intercede in serious situations about nine out of ten times. But there are times when you don't need guarding. During those periods, I see nothing, I hear nothing. You are on your own then. Do you get my drift?"

I did. When I want to be alone, when I need to be alone, when my sense of dignity commands it, when my need for privacy requires it, Paul tunes me out. Or maybe he even goes elsewhere. Even the president of the United States is left alone by the Secret Service during private moments. Paul's reassurances in this respect put my mind at rest and helped me to relax, particularly during those periods when I am behind closed doors with the drapes drawn and the rest of the world is shut out.

Observation By Paul

"The nonbeliever who acts as though God is watching is nobler than the believer who pays no heed."

my hero

Over the months I would learn that Paul had saved my life on more than one occasion, and had pulled me from harm's way dozens of times over my lifetime. He had not only prevented me from being injured physically, but emotionally, financially, and psychologically as well.

I was fascinated by his comment that he gets involved about ninety percent of the time in serious situations. What about that other ten percent of the time when I need his help but he doesn't offer it?

Well, into every life a little rain must fall.

I never asked, and to this day can't imagine why the question never occurred to me then, but I simply assumed that everyone has about the same amount of protection as I have—a 90:10 ratio. That means that no one—prince or pauper, patrician or plebian—gets through life unscathed. No matter how well protected, no matter how privileged, everyone suffers some degree of physical, psychological, emotional, spiritual injury throughout life.

In a memorable query about Paul's appearance in one of my previous books, a Russian immigrant taxi driver in New York wrote to ask me if everyone has a guardian angel. At the time I didn't have the answer, but I told him that even if that were so, it would still be a good idea for him to stop at red traffic signals. A belated answer to this cabby's question would be: Yes, everyone has a guardian angel. But it would be extremely foolhardy to use that information to justify a dangerously erroneous belief that one is invincible, as a result. People with guardian angels get sick, they get hurt, and they die at the rate of two million a year in the United States alone. Ultimately, we are each responsible for our own behavior. If a spirit guardian happens to extricate us from a threatening situation nine times out of ten, let us consider ourselves fortunate. But who among us is perceptive enough to know where and when that intercession will occur?

It could happen while we are sky-diving, or when we are caught by the boss going through private papers on his desk when we thought he was out of the building. Yes, the latter caper, which might appear as harmless curiosity to some, also has the potential to cause devastating effects upon lives.

For instance, at the *Los Angeles Times* on Sundays, during down times on the desk, copy editors used to gather in the managing editor's office during football season to watch games on his color television set. There were usually no high-ranking bosses in the newsroom at the time, so the atmosphere was pretty informal. I wasn't particularly interested in the games, but I would join the others just for the camaraderie.

About four or five years after I joined the *Times*, I was sitting at the managing editor's desk one Sunday afternoon watching a game when my eye wandered to the work baskets on the executive's desk. There was a lone multi-paged document in one of the baskets and, being the curious sort, I naturally took a gander at it.

Lo and behold if I hadn't stumbled upon one of the most tightly guarded secrets at the *Times*! It was a copy of the payroll records for the entire newsroom, listing current salaries, the previous year's merit raises, and recommended raises for that year. The document contained a checklist column for the managing editor to approve, disapprove, or revise those recommendations.

What a revelation it was. I could see immediately who were the highest paid reporters, editors, and copy editors, and there were some startling surprises. For instance, there were only a handful of women copy editors on the main news desks (National, Foreign and Metro)—maybe four or five—and they were all at the bottom of the salary list.

The office political implications would be staggering if this information ever got out. Some of the real workhorses on the reporting staff were drawing salaries well below those of others who were not particularly productive but were well connected politically and personally in the paper hierarchy. In some cases, there was a wide disparity in salary between reporters of equal rank (that is, in terms of abilities, productivity, and seniority), while there appeared to be a correlation between salary and political connections within the office.

If I were a member of management I would be aghast if that information got out. From the perspective of the working stiffs in the newsroom, the salary structure would be viewed as teeming with inequities, definitely unbalanced, and certainly crying out for some sort of modification—a fine-tuning, if you will.

Well, somehow a copy of the document did get made and a week or so later various members of the newsroom staff—about twenty of them—began receiving bulky envelopes through the mail.

I rather imagine that the culprit—whose identity I can attest with absolute certainty—really had little or nothing to gain from the deed. So I would have to infer that he (or she, but let's assume it was a male) was simply playing a little prank while caught up in a moment of devilish madness. There's no doubt that it could have blown up in his face, however, if he got caught.

The response was immediate. The *Times's* photocopy machines went into overdrive as the twenty or so copies suddenly multiplied by the dozens. There probably wasn't a person in the newsroom who didn't have a copy—or certainly access to one—within a day or two. And the newsroom was in an uproar.

Everybody was comparing his or her salary to everybody else's and all but the highest-paid were screaming to their bosses. Discontent was rampant. The women were outraged over what they perceived, and rightfully so, as gender discrimination. Ranking officials from the managing editor down to the city editor were on the defensive, having been put in the extremely uncomfortable and untenable position of trying to explain to some of their best people why this slob or that slouch was making more money than they were.

To prevent a rebellion in the ranks, the *Times* found it necessary to adjust the salaries of scores of people, and I wouldn't be surprised if the total was several hundred thousand dollars annually. That would be millions of dollars over the years. Whatever it was, it had to be substantial.

A deputy managing editor who was not particularly popular in the newsroom was put in charge of the investigation to try to find the source of the leak. He spent months pursuing leads, so it was quite apparent that the company desperately wanted to catch the culprit. I went about my job greatly amused by all of the commotion around me. I suspect that investigation went on for a long time behind the scenes.

I overheard an animated conversation one day between

the city editor and several subordinates. He proclaimed that as soon as the perpetrator was found, he was going to fire him and then punch him in the mouth. I was pretty sure that a nerve had been touched.

Speculation in the newsroom continued for years. Several reporters came under suspicion but the investigation led nowhere and finally ground to a halt.

I had always thought that they hadn't even come close to finding the guilty party because the managing editor's office remained unlocked on weekends, and we copy editors continued to gather there for the televised football games. But in reality, according to Paul, the investigation eventually focused almost exclusively upon me!

Now that came as a shocking surprise. I had never known until that moment that I had been a suspect. Just the thought of it gave me the heebie-jeebies. If they had pinned that rap on me, made me the fall guy, I could have lost everything. I literally had only recently, at that time, made it to what I considered the top of my profession, as high as I could reasonably expect to go based upon my limited education, experience, and abilities. My goal had been to serve securely in that position for the next thirty or thirty-five years, drawing what to me was a munificent salary and being provided with comfortable working conditions, an adequate retirement and health insurance system, and a job that I truly enjoyed.

There was no other way for me to go except down if I failed to hang onto that position. In addition, I had been married for just a few years, had a new baby, and had recently purchased a house in the suburbs. Whatever would possess me to jeopardize all of that for some silly stunt? How could they even *think* such a thing?

The additional money that the *Times* felt obliged to spend on higher salaries was going into the pockets of my brothers and sisters in the newsroom. I like to think that the rascal responsible had served as their unofficial labor representative who had taken it upon himself to help win additional benefits for them through unconventional, unilateral bargaining. It wasn't as if he had sabotaged the presses and cost the company millions of dollars in unnecessary expenses.

No one forced the *Times* to adjust the salaries. If it felt inclined to do so, one could interpret this as an admission that it had been shortchanging those employees. Personally, it didn't matter to me because my pay wasn't adjusted.

Now, as to why I became a prime suspect: It seems that the head of the investigation had recruited one of his minions to snoop around and report back to him regularly with any intriguing scuttlebutt. When Paul informed me of this on that dark night in my back yard thirty years later, I recalled that one of my very good friends at the paper probably did see me at least leafing through the documents. I also was aware that he could have leaped to conclusions if he had seen me at the photocopy machine later performing some innocent little task.

But this was a dear friend of mine and even though I was fond of him, I have to admit that he was a bit of a gossip. In retrospect, I should have known that it was too much of a juicy tidbit to keep to himself during that period when the incident was the talk of the newsroom.

My friend liked to end the day at the local watering hole, as did so many others in the newsroom, and it was there one evening when his well-oiled tongue slipped up. I don't know if the newsroom louse was present, but it would have been just a matter of time before the word would have been whispered to the oily quisling. The little rat heard the rumor and went squealing to the editor investigating the matter, according to Paul.

"Your friend remained loyal," Paul replied. "He was

mighty scared, but he held firm and denied knowing anything about the matter."

"But they knew that he had been talking in the bar, didn't they? Weren't there witnesses?" I asked.

"They put pressure on others who they believed were there and heard the story told by your friend," Paul said. "Not one of them talked. That kind of loyalty says a lot about the person to whom it is applied."

"Then again, maybe they were the ones who got raises and thought, however erroneously, that they had me to thank. Maybe they figured they owed me a favor," I replied with a grin.

"Nevertheless, you still nearly got caught."

"You mean blamed," I protested.

Paul just gave me one of those looks, the sideways glance over the shoulder and down the nose that oozes incredulity and proclaims: "End of discussion."

How much influence Paul had in keeping the hammer from coming down on me—or in assuring that my friend would not buckle to finger me after his barroom gossiping—was not discussed, but the mere fact that he brought up the subject indicates that he had played some role.

Although he either mentioned or at least hinted at a fair number of incidents in which he had been actively involved in keeping me safe from my own foolish self, I got the distinct impression, during our many months of discussions, that I will probably never know the true measure of his contributions.

Here's another example: I have been haunted by a dreadful fear of flying ever since I enthusiastically took my first flight, in a single-engine plane, in the mid-1950s. After that, I flew when I absolutely had to, but avoided it whenever possible. Even though intellectually I knew that flying is really quite a safe mode of travel, I simply could not control my physical and psychological reactions whenever I got on a plane—I was just overcome with trepidation and rode from takeoff to landing in a white-knuckle mode. But again, Paul waved his magic wand, metaphorically speaking, and, presto, it ceased to be a problem—banished. This was probably about 1998. He had predicted that I would be doing quite a bit of air travel sometime soon and thought it best that I be comfortable in that environment.

Now that I had gotten him to talk about his role, he mentioned some other factors in my life that he had also influenced in little ways that radically changed my life.

Up until that point I believed that blind luck was responsible for my being hired by the *Times*. The city's only other metropolitan daily, the Hearst's *Herald-Examiner*, was in the midst of a massive strike when I applied. I really didn't expect to be hired because literally dozens, if not hundreds, of experienced, capable, talented writers and editors were out on the streets of L.A. at the time and many of them were also flooding the *Times* with applications. The working conditions were superior and the pay scales were unmatched anywhere in the western United States.

Job applications by writers and editors from across the country typically were so numerous that I used to joke that the company didn't count them, they weighed them. Somehow, at the very moment that the copy desk supervisor needed to hire a replacement copy editor, my application luckily was sitting on the top of the pile. Fortunately, I lived in the area so there would be no relocation problems or expenses for the company, and I was available immediately. One phone call from him and I was off to his office, lickety-split.

Some years after I was hired, I happened to see the

stack in the supervisor's desk drawer. And, no, I wasn't snooping. He showed the applications to me.

Observation By Paul

"An honorable stranger makes better company than a questionable friend."

times were good

Upon reflection, I suppose I may have given Paul reason on occasion to sincerely believe that I needed to talk, although I continued to reject the idea that I was in a delicate psychological or emotional state. As the song goes, everybody hurts . . . sometimes. I was no exception, but it wasn't anything that I couldn't deal with, in my opinion. However, much as we disagreed on this subject, I certainly wasn't going to tell him to get lost. Our meetings were just too much fun—as well as entertaining, educational, and enlightening. They livened up my days, and I always eagerly looked forward to the next one.

We had been sitting in my gazebo late one afternoon when I expressed concern that one of my neighbors might quite innocently peer over the fence and see me apparently talking to myself. I suggested that we drive to a local shopping center to continue the discussion. I suppose I could have asked him to transmogrify into publicly visible mode, but then that wouldn't satisfy my real reason for proposing the move—my sweet tooth had kicked in and I was hankering to indulge it with some See's candy.

This particular shopping center featured a few benches placed strategically along the length of its concourse and we made use of them when we weren't ambling. Naturally, Paul took on his incarnate form. The subject, which I had initially raised, hadn't changed: We had been discussing the level of misery and wretchedness in the world. It was my contention that no single human being had the capacity to empathize with all of the literally billions of people whose existence consisted of chronic pain, sorrow, squalor, disease, hunger, despair. One lone individual could absorb only so much of others' misery before the mind would collapse under the burden. And so we each do what we can to ease the suffering of a minuscule portion of those in need—by tendering a dollar to a homeless person, visiting a children's hospital bearing gifts, donating to a charity, volunteering to call bingo at a retirement center, offering some kind of helping hand wherever and whenever we are able.

The effort required to pity all of the world's people who deserve our compassion would wrench out the heart, wringing dry the psyche of the most robust person, I argued. It would require a superhuman—or supreme—being. And if such a being existed, then it surely would follow that this entity also would possess the power to prevent, or at least ameliorate, the rampant misery. Ergo, why does such wretchedness exist?

"I know where you're going with this," Paul said. "I'm sorry, but I can't provide you with the answer."

"So you don't know either," I responded, perhaps with just a hint of bitterness.

"I didn't say that. I said I can't give you an answer. Keep in mind that it is not my role to try to remove your doubts."

It seemed that was the end of the exchange, and I wasn't in the mood to bicker. I wondered if I had gotten the right message, that he *can't* provide me with an answer, not that he didn't *know* the answer. I didn't press the issue, and changed the subject—at least tangentially.

"I handled some pretty important news stories when I worked at the *Times*—read them, made corrections, then wrote headlines for them. Some really big stories," I said. "Do you know what stories were the hardest for me to work?" I asked as I savored the richness of the chocolate and the sweet, yummy taste of the nougat. Paul had declined my offer of one of the sugary treats.

"Yes, I do," he replied.

That surprised me. I had asked it rhetorically, as a segue into my intended next statement, but his answer broke the link and I was obliged to change course momentarily.

"Really," I said with a hint of skepticism. I didn't give it the inflection of a question, so it was obviously a bit of a challenge.

"Not the great issues of politics, war and peace, earthquakes, brutal weather, that sort of thing. It was the ones about the suffering of children—some big stories, but many of them just little filler items with tiny headlines," he said.

He was right. I don't know how he knew, but he did. Children are stolen, beaten, molested, murdered, starved, locked in cages, subjected to more forms of cruelty than a healthy brain can ever imagine. And more often than not, the monsters who inflict this suffering upon their defenseless victims are the very ones to whom the children look for safekeeping—their caregivers, often the parents themselves.

Every so often one of these stories leaps to prominence on the front pages, especially when the beast who gets his hands on the child is a stranger. But usually the stories appear as small items on the inside pages—perhaps because they are less titillating; there is no mass hysteria, no fears that a maniac is on the loose in the neighborhood. Not to worry—it was, after all, just a family member who committed the atrocity.

To me, the stories were never routine, no matter how little play they got in the paper. I couldn't help but identify with the battered, murdered, or tortured child.

"Was that a lucky guess, or did I give it away somehow?" I asked.

"Those were the only times I ever saw you cry at work," he said, "a dead giveaway."

I had been studying my shoelaces, my chin resting on my cupped hands, elbows on my knees. The words brought me back from my wanderings and I turned my head to make eye contact. He had to be kidding but I didn't detect any sparkle of humor in the blue eyes.

"Cried? I never cried at work," I said, taken aback by the remark. "Where do you come up with such stuff? Boy, that would make for a joyful newsroom, wouldn't it? Everybody crying whenever a sad story came across the desk. To paraphrase Tom Hanks, there's no crying in the newsroom. Or in the police station either, for that matter."

"Okay, maybe *cried* is a bit of an overstatement. But you certainly misted up on more than one occasion. So your feelings surfaced, so what? I don't see anything wrong with that."

"You know what? I don't think I want to talk about this anymore," I said, unable to keep the annoyance out of my voice.

He just shrugged, as if to say, "No problem, if that's what you want." We took up other subjects until I headed back to the house and Paul went wherever he goes when he goes.

I admit to having a tender spot in my heart for children. Now does that make me a freak of some sort? I suspect that the trait is hard-wired into the very essence of most humans. I also don't like the whole concept of spanking or any other type of corporal punishment.

I'm talking here about children, of course, and not about some sexy lady dressed in black leather cracking a consenting adult on the backside with a horsewhip. Maybe that is a delight for some people but—call me a curmudgeon—I'm more low-key in my tastes.

Spanking—and I use the term loosely to include any kind of hitting of a child, be it a swat on the behind or a smack in the face—is the deliberate infliction of physical pain in an effort to control or modify the behavior of the child. I suppose there are elements of punishment in there somewhere, and efforts to teach the child a lesson, but the bottom line still consists of pain.

At least that's the way I look at it.

I think a "timeout," a temporary loss of privilege—grounding, no TV—or some other form of sanction is more appropriate. But for those who believe in and practice spanking, I would like (ironically speaking) to offer a few suggestions.

There should be standards to control the degree of pain based upon the severity of the child's infractions, the different tolerances and thresholds for pain that each child possesses, and the amount of behavior control that is desired.

For instance, wouldn't it be unreasonable to administer the same level of discomfort to a child for using foul language as for stealing a car? Of course. And then there is the matter of the size and strength of the person administering the punishment. If Momma is five feet two inches and weighs 105 pounds, and Pop is six feet two and weighs 240 pounds, the difference in the amount of pain administered is going to vary greatly between the two.

It would be inherently inequitable for Momma to spank the strapping sixteen-year-old son for car theft while Pop administers the punishment to the frail nine-year-old sister who used the dirty word, right?

The punishment should be tailored to the child by removing the inequities. I suggest to child-hitters that they should construct a simple electrical device that would deliver a shock through electrodes attached to the boy's testes or to the girl's earlobes. A rheostat switch with gradations between one and ten would carefully control the amount of pain, from a mild sizzle to a mind-numbing jolt.

Use a cuss word, get a No. 1 shock. Fight at school, get a No. 5. Steal a car, a No. 10.

It's pretty apparent that certain adults don't consider themselves failures as parents when they turn to violence against their children. Surely it's not because they lack the wisdom, the emotional stability, and the intelligence to find alternatives, right? After all, they were probably raised the same way, and it didn't do them any harm. Look how well they turned out.

However, I wonder if a bit of hypocrisy might be involved. If this behavior modification therapy works on children, it should also work on wayward neighbors, friends, acquaintances, elderly mothers and fathers, wives, husbands. Heck, even the boss could probably use a good thumping occasionally when she gets out of line.

But it's probably a moot point because when the boy grows bigger and stronger and decks the old man with a solid right cross or when the girl gets fed up and runs off with her 16-year-old boyfriend, the parents can take satisfaction in a job well done.

I did not discuss this with Paul.

Observation By Paul

"To be truly appreciated, music must be heard with the heart as well as the ears."

dirty linen

The invitation to my family reunion arrived at a curious time. Paul and I had been discussing my early years. To me it was more akin to reminiscing, and Paul's familiarity with the events of those years also fortified my growing belief that he really had been at my side all of my life, as he claimed.

The reunion was being planned for June of 2002 by members of my extended family in my small Eastern hometown. I had had only minimal contact with any of the dozens of blood relatives—uncles, aunts, cousins, nieces, nephews—in the fifty years since I left for California, which was only slightly less than I'd had with my parents (while they were alive) and my siblings.

First, nearly 3,000 miles separated most of them from me. Second, I had been exposed as a kid to my fair share of the negative dynamics that cause so much stress and dissension within extended families so that I developed a sort of defensive tendency to remain aloof. As a consequence, although I don't believe I consciously made the decision to do so, I was inclined to keep my distance, both literally and figuratively.

Paul and I agreed that my family is not unique. The dynamics of which I speak—gratuitous advice, backbiting, rumor-mongering, feuding, gossiping, and generally sticking one's nose where it doesn't belong—are an integral part of many extended families, my empirical evidence tells me. I need not feel particularly guilty just for remaining detached, he assured me. After all, familial feuding, fussing, and fighting go back a long time.

"Certainly you must know the story of Cain and Abel," he said.

Ah, yes, the original dysfunctional family, I mused silently.

"Sort of. Didn't one of them hit the other with the jawbone of an ass or something like that?" I replied with a straight face.

"Close enough," Paul said, refusing to rise to the bait.

Despite the myths about the historical strength and closeness of the family unit, families in every culture throughout the world are quite commonly and regularly fractionalized by real and imagined hurts and snubs. Misunderstandings, social blunders, and words spoken in anger or under the influence of intoxicants at family gatherings have been known to cause rifts that span decades and lifetimes, Paul told me.

For those cynics who believe that the world is mad, I suppose it can be an amusing spectacle to watch from the sidelines the intriguing interplay between various members of extended families as factions form, divide, shift, regroup, split off, die out, or are resurrected in an ever-changing cycle of metamorphosis. There is probably no end to the pettiness, the jockeying for position, and the recruitment of moral supporters in the really dysfunctional family.

A death in a family can set off a monumental battle when inheritable money or property is at stake, especially when the dear departed one leaves intestate (that is, without a legal will). We've seen it on TV, in movies and in books—therefore it must have some entertainment value—when purportedly loving relatives turn one against the other in a scratching, biting, hair-pulling brawl—figuratively speaking, but often literally—for a share of the loot. My origins are of such a humble nature that there's little to fight over, but I've seen it in other families. And who hasn't read about such conflicts in newspapers? It makes a great story.

When I was a teenager—Paul said I was 15, and I took his word for it—I innocently carried home a bit of backbiting gossip I had overheard at a relative's home. Not really knowing what the comment meant, I repeated it to my mother during some innocuous banter. It involved an unattractive personal characterization made by someone on my father's side of the family about someone on my mother's side.

Paul seemed to know most of the details as I related the story. Sometimes I wondered why I even bothered to tell him about incidents in my life. But I must admit that narrating such experiences was therapeutic at times; I'm sure he was keenly aware of that.

My mother exploded when she heard the remark, her sister who was visiting from California at the time broke down in tears, and I was grilled extensively for all of the sordid details. My hapless father—who was always very close to his parents and his siblings—got both barrels when he walked into the house after work. He did the only thing he could think of when facing a crisis such as this. He berated me mercilessly and threatened to whale the tar out of me for stirring up trouble.

Well, at least it introduced me to a familiar concept that I would deal with on a regular basis in my future career—kill the messenger if you don't like the news.

Memories going back more than sixty years suddenly took on a new and refreshed vitality as I spoke with Paul.

There were a lot of good times when I was growing up, but the things I chose to talk about with Paul tended to drift toward the dark and bleak episodes in my childhood, the stories spilling out with a passion that surprised even me. Paul merely listened quietly.

When I moved to California at age seventeen, I essentially lost contact with most of my assorted kin. In the meantime, there were numerous new additions to the extended family whom I never met.

I did not return when my parents and a brother died back there several decades later. I had become estranged from my adopted sister and I did not even learn of her death until several months afterward.

Yet with all the distance of time and space, the conversation with Paul revealed to me that some memories are too vivid to be forgotten.

Like most families, mine had its share of skeletons in the closet. But it wasn't until I became an adult that I started accidentally discovering them.

Paul listened intently as I talked about these matters, and even encouraged me at several points to delve into as much lurid detail as I cared to and could recall, even though he was quite familiar with my history. I must admit yet again that this opening made possible a certain cathartic release for me. I talked myself out to my heart's content, hashing and rehashing certain elements that particularly galled me. I related familial sagas of betrayal, intrigue, threatened lawsuits, calls for reprisals, wounded relationships, name-calling, bitter physical confrontations, and broken communications in which once-close individuals stopped speaking to one another. I expressed a range of emotions from anger to disappointment, from amazement to outrage, and everything in between. And then Paul seemed to make a point of using the stories to stress a few observations of his own.

"There's an important message here that I want you to keep in mind," he said. "People are not always who they say or believe they are. Rarely are they what others think they are."

It seemed to me that he was stating the obvious.

I should have known better than to underestimate him. His words took on a dramatic, prophetic meaning a few months later, and it was then that I realized why he was so intent on having me bear in mind that simple homily.

Observation By Paul

"The journey began before you were born,
so you are not responsible for where you
started, only for where you go."

Shades of Rod Serling

The night sky in Los Angeles is not ideal for star-gazing. The glow from the city lights can be seen from an airplane a good 250 miles away. However, in my neighborhood about thirty-five miles from the downtown Civic Center, a few hundred stars and some of the planets of our solar system are visible on clear nights despite the corruption of the city lights. I enjoy lounging in the backyard and contemplating the cosmos when conditions are right.

My interest in the heavens has taken on a much sharper focus in the last few years. I had long instinctively suspected that humans are not alone in the cosmos, primarily because the place is too big not to have other life. How can an ocean have only one species of fish?

This belief was magnified enormously when I watched the PBS series *Cosmos* back in the early 1980s, hosted by a handsome, charismatic young man named Carl Sagan. I wondered how anyone could watch that magnificent, awe-inspiring series exploring the vastness and richness of the universe and not believe, or at least imagine, that the cosmos just has to be teeming with other intelligent life.

And then Dr. Sagan himself, a renowned astronomer—a *scientist*—blasted me off the couch when he himself speculated that there might be untold civilizations out there. I could ask for no better validation to support my beliefs than that. I was sold and I had a new hero, a man just five days older than myself.

Despite my beliefs, however, I had never paid much attention to reports of UFOs and the purported presence of intelligent extraterrestrial visitors. While I was convinced that there was a reasonable possibility that we humans share the universe with others, I never felt that there was compelling scientific evidence to support a belief that any of those cosmic neighbors had come a-calling.

I suddenly changed my mind about that in June of 1997, as I have recounted in detail elsewhere. I now firmly believe that extraterrestrials have visited the Earth, continue to maintain a presence in our solar system, and probably have done so for many centuries. In fact, the events that precipitated the radical change in my belief system also were directly responsible for my becoming aware of Paul when I first came face to face with him in a park in Northern California on Easter Sunday in 1999.

So it was no surprise that Paul found me out in the back yard early one balmy night shortly after our intense discussion about my relationships with my family and the secrets that had been revealed. I was lying back in a deck chair staring straight up at the night sky letting my imagination play with fantastic scenes of other families living their lives in faraway civilizations.

By this point, either Paul had miscalculated the depth of the funk in which he had originally thought I was mired, or I had made exceptionally fast progress. Whatever the case, it was only a matter of months after he began seeing me on a regular basis that he determined such sessions were no longer necessary. However, I found the meetings with him so rewarding—and I suspect that he also might have drawn some enjoyment from them—that I prevailed upon him to let us continue. He saw no harm in such an arrangement, and so we agreed to keep it going for an indefinite period of time.

I looked forward to that because I liked him as a friend and a mentor and I truly enjoyed his company. Even though we had agreed that I was no longer in need of professional counseling, there were still times when a simple conversation somehow transformed itself into an informal talk-therapy session. And this evening became one of them.

"Whatcha looking at?" he asked as he settled into a patio chair beside me. I had reached a point where I wasn't always startled when he made an unannounced visit. In fact, there were times and situations when I fully expected him to show up and was surprised when he didn't.

Paul was intimately familiar with my belief in extraterrestrial civilizations so I was quite comfortable in telling him that I was trying to imagine the billions and billions of souls (I use the term loosely) that might be going about their everyday business at that very moment on millions of other planets in the universe.

He joined me at gazing into the night sky.

"Yes, it's a breathtaking and fascinating scene to imagine," he said.

At least five minutes passed in total silence as we pondered the night sky and the wonderful secrets that it surely enveloped in its black satin shroud.

"Do you want to go take a quick peek?" he asked finally, breaking the silence.

"Sure, I'm game. You go bring the spaceship around and

I'll tell my wife that I'll be back in a little while," I said with a chuckle. He smiled, and laughed lightly.

"Well, imagination can transport a person to more wondrous places than any device ever invented by mere mortals."

I hesitated. I had no idea what he had in mind, but my imagination was already at work conjuring up all kinds of epic scenarios.

For no specific reason that I could put my finger on—whether it was merely random or was triggered by something said—I was suddenly in the throes of a mild panic attack. Panic attacks are frightening, but I knew what it was, and knew it would pass.

Now, what the hell brought that on? I thought.

I felt vulnerable out in the open, threatened by who-knows-what unseen dangers here in the darkness. It was as though some ancient vestigial instinct had kicked in, telling me to flee. What had triggered such a reaction? I imagined myself wrapped in an animal skin, standing at the mouth of a cave on a starry, moonlit night eons ago, gazing in speechless wonder and trepidation into the night sky. There was danger in the darkness—so many things to dread, so much terror. As a caveman, I would have no language to express it to others or even to silently verbalize it to myself, but my guts would tell me to withdraw into the relative safety of the cave with the other members of my clan. We would huddle together for warmth and security, and sleep if possible, until the light of a new day broke on the horizon. That welcome sight would help to dispense enough of the numbing fear that lurked in the night to allow the clan to hunt and gather food for the day.

"Come on, don't be nervous," Paul said. He was ribbing me a bit, and yet I got the impression that he could read every detail of thought in my mind by the look on my face. "Besides, it's part of the learning process. Trust me."

He explained that even though he was planning a journey for us, it would be a journey of imagination, as Rod Serling would say in describing *The Twilight Zone*. I would remain safely in my back yard, and yet I would experience a marvelous adventure by simply relaxing in my chair. I agreed to give it a try.

Paul then had me lie back and relax, and talking softly and soothingly to me, encouraged me to let myself go, turn loose of my will, and put myself in his hands. It seemed as though he were trying to hypnotize me. I was not very encouraged because I have always been a bit skeptical about that subject and never thought I could be hypnotized anyway, even if it was a legitimate mechanism. But I did relax. I could feel myself withdrawing from the sights and sounds around me, almost as though I were falling backward into myself. It was not the least bit frightening, but actually was a rather pleasant sensation.

It was instantaneous. I was sitting in an upholstered chair next to Paul, who also was seated. We were in a very large room, the size of an auditorium, and it was filled with a variety of extraordinary-looking creatures. There seemed to be a social event in progress, although there was no music, just a lot of conversation and apparently friendly interaction. I held a drink in my hand. A sip told me that it was non-alcoholic. This was promising to be everything he said it would be—a marvelous adventure.

And to think it was all taking place in my head. I was mesmerized.

"We're on a spaceship," Paul said to me indifferently, as though he were discussing his lunch. I was not overly concerned or surprised. "Just act natural, as though you attend such functions all the time. Follow my lead. You aren't the only earthling aboard, so no one will pay you any undue attention."

"You're talking as though this were real," I said, "rather than an imaginary situation. I know I must be in a trance. Maybe I should be anxious, but I'm not."

"There's nothing to worry about, of course," he replied. "To maintain the atmosphere though, it's best that we both act as if this were a real situation. It helps to sustain the mood and the illusion."

I had no problem going along with that. So I put on my best ham manner and started to play the role that I thought was expected of me. I would immerse myself in the character and pretend with every emotive instinct I could summon to play my part naturally.

I ran my hands and eyes over my "body," which appeared to be clad in the same clothes I was wearing a few moments earlier in my yard. As I marveled aloud about the magic of the moment, Paul smiled benignly and subtly moved his right index finger to his lips to tell me to stay cool.

"You are here," he said firmly. "Your body is not. This is what's known as an astral journey or visit. This is not a good time to explain. Just trust me."

As I took another sip of my drink—which tasted somewhat like orange, perhaps a touch of cinnamon, and a hint of something delicately zesty that I couldn't identify—Paul was looking across the room and then rose from his chair. He called out but the language was not English.

"There's someone I'd like you to meet," he said to me—in English, of course.

At that, I also rose and turned in the direction of the individual he had hailed.

The creature approaching us was anthropoid and bipedal, about six feet six inches in height, with a slender build. I would estimate its weight on Earth at perhaps 150 to 175 pounds. Its face was not unattractive, with very large, round eyes set far apart that sparkled like yellow amber. The mouth was quite large, but not really disproportionate to the face, with full lips from which shone a set of brilliant white, straight teeth. The nose was thin and elongated, and quite sharply defined, similar to the shape that we humans would describe as aquiline.

The individual had a high forehead and the skull was covered in soft, silken, golden hair that fell to shoulder-length. But that description is a bit misleading, because the shoulders were separated from the head by a somewhat thin but muscular neck that was proportionately longer than a human's.

The golden hair and the white teeth were set against an equally light skin color that would have drawn stares at any beach filled with tanned bodies. I didn't know the gender but this exquisite individual seemed so dainty, so … feminine, I suppose … that I just assumed I was being introduced to a female of her species. She didn't appear to be albino, but if she had lived on Earth one could reasonably conclude that she spent little time in sunshine. Nevertheless, she was a delight to behold.

The torso was quite long in proportion when compared with the human form, and the legs were short when judged by that same human standard. The most striking feature, though, was the length of the arms, which most certainly would reach to below the knees of the truncated legs if fully extended. However, the stranger kept its arms above the waist at all times while I was in its presence.

The thought occurred to me that everything I was experiencing—while being played out in my head—was really created by Paul and planted in my brain like so much seed sown in a farmer's field. I simply lacked the required level of imagination to conjure up the strikingly elegant creature standing before me, nor any of the other elements of the "astral journey," for that matter. The person was dressed in a one-piece outfit that covered the area from the collarbone to the ankles and wrists, and seemed to conform pretty closely to the shape of the body, which I had already guessed to be female. The material appeared to be some kind of cloth but it had a sheen and the color was a dark violet or purple.

Paul spoke to the individual in that same foreign tongue, and the stranger replied.

"This is *Grace*," Paul said to me. "She is one of the few people on the ship whose name can be literally translated from her native language to English. Her name means beauty and charm, so Grace is the appropriate translation."

To my surprise, Grace spoke fairly decent English and we exchanged pleasantries. The following exchange is the gist of our brief conversation.

"Oh, a beam rider," Grace said, flashing an amused smile. "Did you enjoy it?"

I looked dependently at Paul. He understood my look of incomprehension and proceeded to explain. A so-called "beam rider" is someone who is moved from one place to another by teleportation, the movement of matter through space by transforming it into energy and then reconverting the energy back into matter again at the terminal point. Some people refer to it as being beamed from point A to point B, thus the term "beam rider."

"He wasn't beamed up," Paul explained to Grace. "We're actually on an astral visit. We'll just be staying for a few minutes and then we have to get back."

"Well I'm sorry you can't visit longer. It's always nice to meet new people," she said to me.

"Some of my people, mostly youths, take beam rides just

for recreation," she said. "They think it's fun. I think it's kind of immature, but it's a harmless practice. They grow out of it."

"Well, some of my people—and not just kids—jump off high towers and bridges attached to a giant rubber band. I think it's insane," I responded, keeping up the pretense that I was in a real situation rather than a fantasy. But it was terrific fun and I went along with it enthusiastically. "I'll take beam-riding over bungee-jumping anytime," I added.

We chatted amicably for about five minutes, after which Grace said goodbye and returned to the group across the room. It consisted of several obviously different species.

"Where's she from?" I asked, continuing the charade.

Paul responded in the same mode, telling me that Grace comes from one of the galaxies in the group of galaxies known as the Virgo supercluster, the same one to which the Milky Way and our nearest neighbor galaxy, Andromeda, belong. I know almost zip about astronomy or the heavens, although both hold a fascination for me, and it is too late in life for me to begin a study of this subject; but if I understood him correctly, the supercluster contains about 3,000 galaxies and is about 100 million light-years across. If so, that means that Grace, if she were real, would be a neighbor, although I never learned whether she would be a close neighbor or a more distant one.

Grace would be the equivalent of a human young adult, perhaps eighteen to twenty years old in human terms, although her chronological age in Earth years would be closer to forty, Paul said. I had to give him credit; he didn't get out of character for even a moment, never made the tiniest slip. He was inside my head, and yet he never once gave any indication of that, completely giving himself over to the role.

"She has been aboard for about five Earth years and probably will leave the ship and return home in another year or two. She is one of several hundred such exchange students aboard, representing almost as many different species," he said.

"So, what's in her future? Finish her schooling, begin a career, get married, have kids, buy a house in the suburbs?" I asked whimsically. To my surprise, Paul gave me a straightforward answer to my frivolous remark.

"Pretty much so. However her people don't have marriage. She'll likely take a mate and get a house in the suburbs, as you so quaintly put it. But it's unlikely that she will have children. What would you say if I told you that she's a homosexual?"

I stared at him dumbly. Then I blinked. I remember trying to maintain a detached look, as if to say *you can't shock me*, but I'm sure all kinds of emotions were doing a lively dance across my face. I casually glanced over my shoulder toward Grace, shifted the weight on my feet, temporizing as I groped for the words that would constitute an appropriate response. It was useless.

Hot darn, this was so much fun. I was having a magnificent time. If I was nonplused, something positive did emerge from the moment, however. His sense of humor was showing. Paul locked eyes with me and I could see his face doing a frolicsome dance, and he was enjoying it immensely.

"You know, if you had a Star Trek phaser, you could save a lot of words by zapping me with that," I said. "It wouldn't be any more stunning than these periodic zingers you keep hitting me with."

The mock gaze of bafflement didn't fool me. He was still playing the game.

"Oh," he said after a moment's silence, "the space fantasy on your television and movie screens. How have I stunned you?"

"The gay thing!" I fairly blurted in embellished exasperation. He knew he had jolted me but he feigned innocence as though he couldn't imagine what might bring on such a reaction. I admit that he had me off balance. I wondered if he was smiling inwardly. Sometimes I couldn't tell when he was serious or merely tweaking my nose playfully. Perhaps it was a combination of both.

"Of course," he said. "Many humans still haven't come to grips with that aspect of their physiological diversity. Well, no matter. Those homophobic demons will someday be exorcised. It's just a matter of time—and education."

Homosexuality is rare in the universe simply because of the scarcity of wide-ranging diversity among most species, Paul said. He added, to my amazement, that it is more common among humans than any other species. Paul went on to explain that there are a number of species that, while nowhere near as disparate as the human race, are not totally homogenous, and it is in these cultures that homosexuality is present in limited forms. It is simply accepted as a normal part of the physiological tapestry of the species.

"Don't tell me you're a homophobe," Paul said. Did his tone indicate suspicion? No, he was still teasing. "I'd be very surprised if I was mistaken about you to that degree."

"Not at all," I replied. "I believe in live and let live. However, the Christian Bible does say it's an abomination," I added.

Again the look—across the shoulder and down the nose. Just what in blazes was that look supposed to mean, anyway? He had a habit of aiming it at me at various times, and I thought I had figured it out. But I wasn't sure now. It seemed to carry a slightly different meaning every time he laid it on me. Skepticism? Mild reproof? No, now I had it. It said, *"And just whom do you think you're kidding with your nonsense?"*

"And how would you know?" he asked.

"Well, uh, I've heard rumors of a sort," I replied. "Anyway, I was joking."

Of course, he was right. I had never read the Bible and he knew it. I actually have two or three of them somewhere around the house but have never been able to get beyond the first three or four pages. It's not exactly a page-turner, to my mind. Besides, the opening doesn't make any sense to me. I figured that if I was lost so quickly into it, I sure wasn't going to be able to follow the plot, so I gave up.

"Do you know that homosexuality has been a part of the human makeup from the time your species first appeared? I'm talking about a very long time," he said.

Another blast from the phaser! No, I didn't know that. I've never given it much thought.

He was right about this being a learning experience. I didn't know if what he was telling me was actual fact or if it was fiction for the sake of the production—the "astral journey"—but it was interesting, nevertheless.

"Do you know where you would be today if all of the contributions that homosexuals have made to human society and culture over the ages were suddenly wiped out?" he asked.

"Bangladesh?"

Again I got the look.

"I'm sorry," I said. "Sometimes I don't know when to keep...."

"No, no, I'm not scolding," he said softly, laying a hand gently upon my shoulder.

"What do I know about such things?" I asked. "I'm not an expert on anything. I'm just a retired newspaperman."

Love and sex are not intertwined among some species as they are in human romantic relationships, Paul went on. I had heard similar theories about love, sex, and marriage several years earlier under quite unusual circumstances. The conversation was almost a rehash of these previous discussions on the subject.

Paul was playing devil's advocate, although I didn't know it at the time, when he went on to suggest that there might be a weakness in the human marriage arrangement.

"And what might that be?" I asked, perhaps a bit defensively.

"It's just a theory, an observation," he replied. "I'll tell you, but I don't want you to take offense. It's not a criticism of your culture."

We were interrupted in our dialogue several times when various individuals, not human as far as I could tell, approached Paul and exchanged words with him. Actually, that's just a wild guess. In reality, they exchanged sounds with him, which I guessed to be words. However, even that was not the case for one odd individual—rather short, no more than four feet tall, under one hundred pounds, bipedal, delicate features, and wearing a wraparound sarong-like garment that covered him or her from neck to ankles; this one stood face-to-face with Paul as though in conversation and yet I heard not a sound. Their visit lasted about two minutes.

My mind was racing in high gear by now. As if this so-called journey weren't uncanny enough, one had to wonder if it wasn't pushing the limits of plausibility to sincerely believe that Paul was creating this whole scenario in my mind. The details alone would leave one breathless. Was it really a fantasy or was it possible that in reality I—the Earth-born person who is *me*—was actually in this place on an astral visit, even as my physical body reposed on the deck chair back home? There's no doubt the situation was surreal; the scene was not exactly dream-like, but it was still lacking just a little bit of that solid, down-to-earth quality of the fully awake state. There may have been slight elements of a fugue or dissociation. If so, it could only be described as a hint of such. Perhaps that's the normal feeling when one is in a trance. I just don't know.

I was pretty sure that my physical body wasn't present. But I couldn't swear to that either! It was downright confusing.

Paul returned to my side.

"You looked like you were speaking," I said.

"Yes."

"I didn't hear a word."

"No, you wouldn't have, it was a private conversation."

"Without words?" I asked suspiciously.

He merely smiled—or was it a Cheshire-cat grin?

"You and I were talking about your marriage customs," he said.

Right. He hoped I wouldn't take offense. I assured him that I lean toward giving all rational ideas and opinions a fair hearing, whether or not I agree. I gave up any thought of asking him how he had communicated with the previous individual, why he hadn't introduced me, or, heaven forbid, what they were talking about.

Then he went off on a long dissertation about the human condition from a universal perspective, rattling off facts and figures and hopscotching from subject to subject, touching on sociology, physiology, religion, and psychology.

People on earth, he said, classify love into two major groups—sexual and non-sexual. These two categories are broken down into two distinct sub-groups—instinctive and purposeful. Because most humans do not hold in their hearts a universal love for all other people—although there are several million idealists who are exceptions—the vast majority selectively personalize love. They choose the people they love—either purposefully or instinctively. Most love of family members such as parents, children, grandchildren, grandparents, and siblings is generally instinctive. These relationships are considered strictly non-sexual.

The lines begin to blur, Paul said, when it comes to the love of more distant relatives such as aunts and uncles, nieces and nephews, and cousins. All of these can be either instinctive or purposeful. These relationships are considered non-sexual, and it is generally taboo—and often illegal—in much of the world for such blood relatives to engage in sexual intimacy.

Love of non-family members, such as best friends, favorite movie stars, heroes of all types, or religious leaders, for example, is categorized as purposeful, Paul observed. That is, the person consciously chooses to love the designated one. It could be argued, though, that the love of a true national icon—such as General Dwight Eisenhower, who led a grateful nation to wartime victory—could be instinctive.

Here again, Paul told me, the lines blur, and the love could be of either a sexual or non-sexual variety. In the case of Eisenhower, it was probably mostly non-sexual. But what of the adoring fans of Elvis Presley? How much of the affection of his millions of admirers, particularly among females, was free of a sexual element?

"I'm trying to follow you," I told Paul, "but I'm not sure where you are going. I'm still looking for the so-called weakness that you see in our marriage customs."

"Do you want it in a nutshell?" he asked.

"Please."

"Humans believe that the tapestry of marriage is woven from the fibers of love. There are those who contend that the whole thing would unravel and fall to the floor in a jumbled heap if somehow nature suddenly drained your reservoirs o certain essential chemicals," he said.

I needed time to digest that. I tried to think of some dilatory maneuverings, but nothing came to mind. I merely stared at Paul. I thought I'd try posturing, but he'd see right through that. Oh, well; if honesty is the best policy, I might as well just get on with it.

"And what conclusions am I supposed to draw from that?" I asked. "I'm not even sure that I would agree with it, even if I really knew what it meant."

That question and statement opened up another floodgate. According to the chemical-deprivation theory, he went on, millions of impending marriages would be called off and even millions of established marriages would crumble. That's because the engine driving those relationships is lust-based rather than love-based, according to some observers. He didn't mention whether these observers were of the human or non-human type.

Naturally, many marriages, the ones that are truly love-based, would remain intact. Loss of libido would certainly wound those particular relationships but they could survive, the theory goes.

"Let me set a scenario for you, and then you tell me if you don't agree that the reasoning processes are bizarre, at the least, if not perverse."

"I'm listening," I said.

"A man professes his undying romantic love for a woman, but she spurns his attention. She has no sexual interest in him. He then decides that if he can't have her, nobody can, and he kills her. Can that truly be someone's idea of love?" he asked.

Millions of women are brutalized daily throughout the world by men who purportedly love them, who are supposed to be their protectors, not their victimizers, Paul continued.

caring so deeply about another individual that a ld go to almost any lengths, make whatever or she is capable of making in good conscience, to ensure the happiness, the well-being, the comfort of the loved one.

"Our hypothetical character that I just described, upon being rejected by the object of his affections, should take the woman's hands in his, look lovingly into her eyes, and tell her that he understands and that he wishes her every happiness in life. And then he should walk away in dignity, hoping with all his heart that life would be good to her," Paul said.

"That is what love is!" he explained. "To deliberately inflict harm, pain, or death upon another in the name of love—or God, for that matter—is an obscenity of incomprehensible proportions. And, of course, it really isn't love. It's lust, obsession, ego—something twisted out of all normal appearance."

He then touched on the high divorce rate among humans, the jealous rages of domestic violence, the devastating effects on children of broken families, and the hateful battles of divorcing couples over community property and custody of children.

I was starting to feel like a mugging victim and I momentarily wondered if he was purposely putting me through an arduous harangue for some cruel reason that I could not fathom. I immediately dismissed the thought because the notion ran counter to everything I knew about Paul as extremely intelligent, highly compassionate, warmhearted, polite, and caring—not to mention that any evidence of unkind intentions on his part would directly contradict what he was in the act of teaching. Infliction of cruelty was not in Paul's nature. And I guess I couldn't even call it a tirade because there really was no emotion displayed. He had merely held a mirror up to me as a representative of my species, and I saw some very ugly truths that I would have preferred not to see.

"Then, are you condemning the human institution of marriage?" I asked.

"Not at all," Paul replied. "Would you ask your mechanic if he was condemning your automobile just because he found a malfunctioning part? Of course not."

"Do you know which of your marriages are the most successful ones, statistically?" he asked, as though not even hearing my question. "I'll tell you—marriages in later life when the flames of passion do not burn with the same intensity as they did in youth. Lust becomes less of a driving force, and the more mature and wiser couple who fall in love do so because they find that they truly like and care about each other as spiritual soul mates and want to travel through their remaining days together."

He was pursuing his point with great enthusiasm. There seemed to be an attitude of ... what? ... certainly not malice or arrogance. Not self-righteousness or smugness. Paul was not trying to disillusion me or force me to admit that his position was right and mine was wrong. Despite what a casual observer might think, the real issue here was not the human marriage custom. That subject was merely the vehicle he was using to achieve his goal. And what was that goal?

The very one that every good teacher shoots for. He was trying to trigger some thinking, to motivate me to reflect, to question. Lovingly and tenderly, he was trying to teach me to challenge accepted concepts so that I would not embrace them simply because they represented popular thought. He wanted me to accept or reject them based upon my own quest for the truth.

A teacher can experience no greater reward than inspiring a student to embark upon a lifelong pursuit of learning in search of truth. Somehow, Paul knew that he had reached me, and he was reveling in the joy of that accomplishment.

So there it was. We really weren't talking about sex, love, marriage, and romance. Those were the topics, but they weren't the real subject. He could just as easily have talked about flower arrangement and taxidermy and still gotten his message across. Paul was merely using those themes as tools to get to the heart of the real issue: the value of independent, reflective thinking. He was a sage, a teacher, and I was the student who had just been put through a grueling lesson.

I could almost feel the wheels of the cerebral mechanism begin to whir as my brain shifted toward a more analytical mode from the one of imagination that had been occupying my time so entertainingly. At the same time, probably because my focus had shifted, I felt the fantasy—trance, delusion, hypnotic spell, whatever one wants to call it—beginning to slip away. And then, in a nanosecond, I was back on my patio chair.

Paul was standing over me, smiling.

"What happened?" I asked, jarred by the suddenness of the transition.

"You broke the spell. It's okay, though. I'm actually impressed because you held onto the suspended state of consciousness much longer than I would have expected. That's unusual for a first experience."

Modesty having never been one of my strong suits, I puffed up a bit upon hearing that news.

"It wasn't very difficult. Acting isn't that hard. It was quite a trip, though," I said. "I can see why some people have a fascination with hallucinogenic and psychedelic drugs. Wow. One thing, though ... "

"Yes?"

"That ... girl ... Grace?"

"Yes?"

"Just out of curiosity, even though she isn't real, why did you make her gay?"

"Just food for thought."

And then he left in his customary manner. I sat alone for a few minutes longer, reliving the experience, cogitating. Was Paul holding something back for some reason? Was it really a journey of the mind, strictly an imaginary excursion? Or was it possible that I had indeed, sans body, traveled to a bona fide place?

I wonder.

Observation By Paul

"Welcome the opportunity to meet new people because a friend can be acquired in no other way. All of your friends were once strangers."

precocious child

I couldn't shake the memory, couldn't get it out of my head. The journey Paul and I had just taken was, to put it in the vernacular of the street, a mind-blowing event. Such simple adjectives as *fantastic, astounding*, or *stunning* simply don't do the proper job of conveying the magnificence and magnitude of it all. It preoccupied me to the point where I had difficulty falling asleep at night. After hours of tossing and turning, I would have to make a conscious effort to clear my mind of all thought so that sleep could set in. The typical period required for most people to fall into deep sleep is approximately seven minutes. Sometimes I would get probably as far as five or six minutes of keeping my mind clear of all thought, only to fall back into thinking about the experience again. And then I had to start all over again, trying to achieve the seven minutes of total mental blankness.

When I met Paul again a few days later, it was my intention to immediately bring the subject around to the astral voyage. I had a million questions that had to be asked or I would explode, I thought. We met, of all places, at a local commuter train station to take a round trip to Los Angeles. It is about a thirty-five or forty-minute ride one way, with the line terminating at the historic Union Station downtown. The station also serves as a major hub for the Metrorail subway system that is methodically and gradually reaching out tentacles along some of the busier commuter destinations throughout the greater metropolitan area.

I arrived at the local station about fifteen minutes early, bought my ticket at the vending machine, and looked about in vain for some sign of Paul. I began to grow a bit anxious as the minutes ticked down to departure time and still caught no sight of him. The rails resonated a barely detectable hum that signaled an approaching train, which moments later lumbered into view in the distance, just about the same time that Paul sauntered up onto the platform in fully embodied form. At least that's the way he appeared to me.

It was late May or early June of 2002, as I recall, a month more or less before the scheduled family reunion.

I was dressed warmly enough to remain comfortable in the morning chill, but still lightly enough that I wouldn't be too uncomfortable if the day turned warm. Paul was dressed in, of all things, a brown suit with tie and was carrying a briefcase, blending in quite well with the eclectic mix of commuters. We made eye contact just about the same moment that someone called out my name as I was about to enter the train to grab a couple of seats for Paul and me.

I turned in the direction of the voice. Scampering into our car was a man who had introduced himself to me several years earlier at an event where I had delivered a talk. Actually, we had hit it off pretty well and became quite friendly, although not to the point where we socialized together. I ran into him periodically in local stores, and we would spend anywhere from fifteen minutes to an entire hour gabbing, depending upon the circumstances. He didn't live near me, but his work brought him to the area on a regular basis.

He was moving quickly toward me, accompanied by a pre-adolescent boy.

"Let's go grab a seat," he said, taking hold of my arm as he entered, practically dragging me along. I looked back helplessly at Paul, who had seen what happened and who followed on our heels. Dave headed for a pair of facing seats on the lower level of the bi-level car. It would be less crowded there and would allow us a greater degree of privacy for conversation. Dave was a hardcore UFO enthusiast and our conversations invariably centered on that topic. In fact, it was difficult to talk about anything else because even a mention of the weather would give him an opening to turn the subject back to UFOs and alien abductions.

He and the boy slid into a seat and I took a facing one. As I was scooting over to the window, Paul made a casual entrance and immediately sat down beside me. He put his "briefcase" on top of the small table that separated the two sets of seats. I nearly gasped.

This was going to be damn interesting, I thought. I fully expected some reaction from Dave and/or the boy, but they expressed none. Even though Paul had arrived on the scene looking to me like just another commuter, obviously he was undetectable to others.

When he hadn't stopped at the ticket vending machine, that should have tipped me off but I didn't make the connection at the time.

Paul winked, gave me a mischievous smile, and faded to an apparition even as the "briefcase" simply disappeared. This was surreal enough to shock even a spiritualist who holds séances, practices voodoo, talks to the dead, or engages in other activities of a mystical, paranormal, or metaphysical nature. For a person such as myself this was almost too much to absorb. The only element that made it tolerable and kept my heart from hammering through my chest wall—it was already halfway into my throat—was that I had been exposed to such a variety and number of paranormal surprises in recent years that I suppose my central nervous system had become somewhat inured to the excitement.

So why even bother fading to an apparition in my eyes? I never got around to asking, but I must admit that he was a less distracting presence in that form, barely detectable in my peripheral vision, in which case my eyes wouldn't keep wandering to him. I suspect that was his purpose. But quite frankly, this habit of his of flitting in and out of his various forms—particularly when he seemed fully incarnate for all to see when in actual fact he was visible only to me, even dressed to the nines—was beginning to wear on my nerves.

The boy with Dave was a handsome young man who appeared to be about twelve or thirteen years old. He had fascinating green eyes that almost seemed to glitter and a shock of light-brown hair just on the shy side of blondish.

With those two features, not unlike those of Nordic types, I would expect a pale skin color, but the child's complexion was a contrasting darker shade somewhere between tan and bronze. The effect was quite striking, and I could imagine that in not too many years he would become the object of many young ladies' attention. He had a dazzling smile that contrasted wonderfully with the pink lips and the bronze skin tones.

"Haven't seen you for a while," Dave said. "Where you heading? The boy and I are just going exploring. I've been busy with work—too busy—and decided to take the day off, spend some quality time together. We were just going to roam around L.A. Oh, this is my son, Marco."

Dave was a non-stop talker. He could bend my ear for hours if I let him and if he had the time. Fortunately, he didn't always have the time, and when he did I usually excused myself after about an hour. I liked him, but his talkative nature did tend to wear a body down after a while. Dave was rather ordinary looking, almost nondescript, probably in his early- to mid-forties. As for the boy, I found myself staring at him and thinking that his mother must be a real looker; I couldn't detect even the slightest resemblance to his father.

"As in *Polo*?" I asked. I had never met anyone named Marco before.

"Correct," the boy said as he reached out a hand to me. He had a surprisingly firm grip that belied both his size and level of maturity as represented by his age. That is, a boy's handshake is often weak and flaccid, an indicator of inexperience and the timidity he feels upon meeting an adult stranger. As he gains maturity and experience, particularly if he's an alpha male, his grip firms up concurrent with his growing confidence in himself. Men who never do develop a firm handshake immediately telegraph to the person they are greeting that they are shy, at the very least, and quite possibly insecure.

I told Dave that I too was just bumming around, taking a day off, although that sounded odd even to my ears because I had been retired for years; as far as the world was concerned, every day for me was a day off. For just a moment, I flashed on the familiar theme of all of the workers on the copy desks back at the *Times* and felt a twinge of sympathy for them, cooped up inside when the outdoors was so glorious. But that thought lasted about a nanosecond. Was I really concerned about a bunch of news wonks who in all likelihood actually preferred to be indoors rather than in the great outdoors? Fat chance.

Dave tried to get me involved in a conversation about UFOs, but I was having none of it this day, so I changed the subject constantly until, for one of the few times that I could remember, he finally gave up on the issue and we passed the rest of the time in idle chatter until we disembarked at Union Station. In the meantime, I had allowed myself to be maneuvered into spending the time with him and his son. I couldn't think of any delicate way to get out of the invitation, and I didn't want to be impolite. I had looked at Paul for some guidance at the time, but he merely shrugged and told me to go ahead, that he would accompany us, and that I might learn something. Naturally, I was the only one who could hear him.

I wanted to ride some of the newer legs of the Metrorail subway system because the network had grown considerably since I last had ridden it and I felt like exploring. However, Dave had other ideas. He preferred to walk, which would also give us a bit more privacy—or so he said softly in an almost conspiratorial voice.

I don't know how many miles we walked, but it was a good workout throughout downtown. Our route took us across Alameda Street to historic Olvera Street, a narrow cobblestone road less than a block long and not much wider than an alley, and crammed with commercial stalls. Tens of thousands, perhaps hundreds of thousands, of tourists descend upon it yearly to patronize its dozens of vendor stalls and restaurants that reflect the Spanish influence on the city.

Olvera Street runs right through the middle of what's known as El Pueblo de Los Angeles, an interesting collection of historical buildings typical of a Spanish village. Such villages usually were anchored by a central plaza, government buildings, and, of course, a church. Mexican ranchero music filled the air as we walked through the plaza.

"Have you ever heard of the term *Star Seed* or *Star Child*?" Dave asked as we began our journey.

He was back on the subject again, but I was in an expansive mood so I resigned myself to the predictable discourse that was to come. I told him that I thought the terms referred to supposedly hybrid children who are the product of a combination of human DNA and extraterrestrial DNA. I've talked to some people who are firm believers in the existence of such hybrids. These reports have been circulating for years, mostly in the New Age and UFO/alien-contact communities, although there have been occasional references to the phenomenon in the mainstream media, including a handful of books by credentialed researchers. Basically, those telling the stories claim that they experienced contact with aliens during which human and extraterrestrial DNA were somehow mixed to produce hybrid children—or at least believed firmly in the existence of such children for one reason or another. Sometimes the humans were said to be donors of eggs or sperm, removed from them voluntarily or taken involuntarily. In other cases, a human female might receive donor alien sperm and actually carry the resultant hybrid child to term, at least according to the theory.

I never paid too much attention to the stories. However, I like to think that I remain receptive to any plausible information that might convince me of the stories' authenticity. After all, it's a big universe, so why not hybrid children? I'm sure there are stranger things going on out there.

"But I must tell you," I said to Dave, "even though I have personally heard a woman at a workshop claim that she was the mother of such an offspring, I've never met a so-called Star Child."

"Really? Say hello to Marco," Dave said.

I stopped dead in my tracks, causing a mini-traffic jam on the narrow street with half a dozen people being forced to stream around me. I knew the kid was unusual, at least in appearance. He hadn't spoken much so far, although what he did say struck me as pretty advanced in both vocabulary and intellectual acuity for a child of his age. At the time, I assumed that he was just another precocious kid. Well, come to think of it, I guess he was. We resumed our walk.

"You're trying to tell me … that …."

"Absolutely. He's a Star Child," Dave said with an approving smile as he laid a gentle and protective hand upon the boy's shoulder.

We exited Olvera Street and continued northward on Alameda toward Chinatown. I worked at trying to hear him out, but I was also reserving judgment about whether I was going to accept his story at face value. After all, it smacked of myth and fiction, a tale more fantastic than any news story I had ever come across during my thirty years in the newspaper business. But at that point in my life I could not dismiss the bizarre notion out of hand because of my recent drastic change in thinking regarding alien life forms.

According to Dave, he and his wife had tried unsuccessfully for years to have a child, and after consulting several specialists they resigned themselves to the fact that the woman was incapable of conceiving. They both were heartbroken. Shortly afterward, the wife had an extraterrestrial contact in which she was given the opportunity to carry her husband's child. Dave would have to donate some semen, which would be used to fertilize a donor egg from an extraterrestrial female that then would be implanted in his wife. The hybrid child would be theirs to raise as their own.

Normally my instinct for being nosy should have demanded at this point that I ask the fundamental questions of who, what, why, when, where, and how, but I didn't. Maybe I really wasn't taking the story seriously yet and was more intent on enjoying the yarn uncritically to see where Dave was taking it. Or perhaps I had simply become so accustomed to hearing tales of extraterrestrial contacts—more than one might imagine—that it does not even raise an eyebrow anymore. Whatever the reason, I don't have any details on who the purported aliens were, what the circumstances of the meeting were, where or when the first contact took place, or why or how this particular woman (Dave's wife) was chosen for the role.

In any case, when offered the opportunity to carry a child, the excited wife talked it over with Dave, and he readily agreed. Arrangements were made and Marco was the beautiful result. Because it was an interspecies transfer, no fertilization could have taken place without some form of genetic intervention. Certain biological procedures had to be performed in order to make the egg and sperm compatible and also to keep the woman's immune system from rejecting the egg. However, the procedure had been devised and perfected many generations earlier, so the process that produced Marco had long before become routine medical practice with this particular alien race. When the boy was old enough to understand the implications, the circumstances of his birth were explained to him.

So far I was unconvinced, but I willingly played along to remain civil and also to encourage Dave to keep talking. It was a fascinating story and I was smitten with curiosity.

"How long ago was that?" I asked.

"What, when he was born?" Dave responded.

"No, dad," Marco interjected, "he means when was I told."

Perceptive kid.

"About a year ago, when I was eight," Marco answered for his father.

"You're only nine?" I asked, taken by surprise. "You seem older. I would have guessed eleven to thirteen."

Dave beamed proudly. There was no doubt that he had bonded with his son, but I wondered how the wife was taking it.

"So you don't know who your biological mother is?" I asked Marco. But before he could answer, I turned to Dave. "Where does he live? Do you take care of him? Are you still married? What does your wife think? How has she adjusted to the situation?"

"Wait. One question at a time," Marco cut in. "Let me answer your first question and then dad can answer the others. No, I don't know who my biological mother is, but as far as I am concerned my real mother is the woman who is raising me, my father's wife. Maybe someday when I reach adulthood I will meet my biological mother, but I have no compelling interest in doing so at this time. Perhaps I'll change my mind. If I do, the search should be relatively routine, because there are records."

I stared in admiration at him. This was definitely one bright kid. I know a lot of adults, probably including myself, who would have a hard time stringing together a series of sentences like that right off the tops of their heads.

"I'm sure dad will fill you in on the rest. I think I'm going to leave now," the boy said.

"Where to?" I asked.

"Exploring, then home," he replied simply. To my amazement, he gave Dave a hug, shook hands with me, said goodbye, and doubled back toward downtown. Dave and I continued our walk toward Chinatown.

"Will he be all right by himself?" I asked as we left Marco.

"He's fine. He's very mature for his age. If he wanted to travel around the world by himself, I wouldn't stand in his way. I'd miss him something terrible, but I wouldn't stop him."

According to the father, the boy is quite independent and capable of taking care of himself, although he lets his parents dote on him as though he were as dependent upon them as any child his age would be. Marco's extraterrestrial mother knows that he exists, and there is a complete file on her as an egg donor in some distant hall of records, including her name, date of birth, planet of birth, species, genealogy for several generations, medical history, and other pertinent information. Or so Dave insists.

I had to admit it was an amusing and entertaining yarn so far.

In answer to the flurry of questions I had fired at Dave right before Marco left, Dave said his wife has bonded with the boy as tightly as any mother could possibly connect with any offspring. She loved him dearly and was totally devoted to him.

I was glad of that.

That was strange, I thought. Why did I feel pleased to hear about the woman's affection for the boy? It was as though I was beginning to believe the story even though I kept telling myself that I was still unconvinced.

By the time we reached Chinatown, I had learned that Marco's biological mother—I don't even know if that is the proper characterization for the female who donated the egg—is humanoid in appearance but whose looks certainly would draw attention on the street because of the dissimilarities between the two species. Nevertheless, I thought, she must be a beauty because Marco got his good looks from somewhere and it certainly wasn't from Dave. When Marco reaches adulthood—and I never learned when that will occur—he will be given the opportunity to meet the female egg donor.

Biologically, would Dave's wife be the "real" mother even as a surrogate who carried the child to term but didn't contribute the egg? I just don't know and I wasn't presumptuous or brazen enough to ask. I suppose there are moral and ethical issues involved. Of course, the question would be relevant only if Dave's story was true. The thought that he could be delusional crossed my mind more than once during our outing.

Marco is one of "thousands" of Star Children, according to Dave. Again, I never could pin down a precise number.

Not all Star Children live on other planets, Dave explained. Sometimes eggs are taken from human females and fertilized with alien sperm, and sometimes sperm is taken from human males and used to fertilize the eggs of alien females; in such cases, the resultant children are more apt to be raised in the alien cultures. On the other hand, sometimes the sperm of alien males is surreptitiously inserted into the eggs of human women, and the offspring are allowed to be born and raised in an Earth culture. In many such instances, the mother has no inkling that her very ordinary human bundle of joy is actually a very extraordinary hybrid Star Child. In other instances, such as Dave's, the mother is fully aware of the process and is a willing subject.

There is a branch of alien science, Dave claimed, that deals with the study of hybrid children who are raised in a variety of cultures. That is, hybrid children who are raised off Earth are contrasted with hybrids who are raised on Earth. The differences between the two and the influences of the cultures and environments that could account for those differences are put under the microscope, figuratively speaking.

This is all according to Dave, of course. It was wacky, but for the time being I was willing to suspend my disbelief and listen objectively. We found a bench on a Chinatown street and sat down to take a breather; we had been walking for quite a while. Tantalizing food smells filled the air, and on decided to enter a nearby restaurant. The tourist season was over, so the vast majority of people who passed us were of Asian descent. Sitting in this crowded spot, it was hard for me not to stare at the young women and girls who strode by. I found myself conflicted at times trying to decide whether to enjoy the sight of them approaching or to turn my attention to the equally appealing sight of them walking away. Either girl-watching or walking—or perhaps both—are strenuous activities because I was suddenly aware that I had worked up an appetite. We entered a cafe.

I sucked down my glass of lemonade before the fried noodles that I had ordered arrived. "You're pretty good with those things," Dave said admiringly, nodding toward the chopsticks that I was using to shovel the noodles into my face. "You don't need a fork, huh?"

He was using a fork.

"Nope," I said between bites. "I only ask for a fork when I have soup. I can't seem to get the chopsticks to work on soup."

Paul, standing nearby, seemed to roll his eyes and I almost expected to hear him groan. Not everyone takes a fancy to my attempts at levity. I find that children seem to appreciate them more than adults.

He looked at me strangely for a moment and then chuckled. After we split the bill we continued our walk. We headed south on Broadway through the Civic Center and down to First Street. I took a walk around the *Los Angeles Times* building. It had been my home away from home for twenty-five years and I must admit to a certain pang of nostalgia. I had spent a lot of good years in that building with a lot of good people. But time brings change, and in the final few years the job had become less fun and less rewarding. Also, the personalities of a few of the new people I had to work with didn't mesh well with mine. I found myself laughing less and less at work. That helped to motivate me to take the early-retirement buyout offer when I was a mere fifty-eight.

Finally, we headed north on Spring Street, cut over to Alameda and returned to Union Station. Although I could see him as an apparition, Paul never said a word to me during those hours, although he had been nearby all of the way. Dave wanted to head back home but I told him I wanted to pay another visit to the *Times*.

"One thing, though, before you go," I said. "Why did you decide to tell me about your son? I mean, I'm sure it's something that you and your family keep a pretty tight lid on. Why me? And why now?"

"You're right, hardly anybody knows. Marco is going to be really successful—when he's an adult, I mean. Well, he's already special. You know what I mean?"

I knew that he was groping for words. I suspect that Dave never went to college. His grammar and vocabulary could have used some improvement.

"Yes, he is an exceptional child," I said, "and I expect that he will become an equally exceptional adult."

"Yeah, that's the word I was looking for, *exceptional*," Dave said. "Do you know that he doesn't have to go to school? He learns everything on his own. Imagine that. He's a—what's the word?—a vivacious reader and very curious. But he'll have to go to college because he'll need the degree to get a job, or get a license to become a professional, or whatever he decides to do with his life."

"Right, voracious," I said as delicately as I could.

"Yeah, that's what I meant."

He still hadn't answered my questions, though, and I brought him back to them.

"Oh, yeah," he said, "it's just that I really trust you. And

I thought you would understand and still keep it to yourself, and not ridicule me or make fun of me. I liked your books, and I knew that I could tell you. Oh, boy, have I wanted to tell someone for a long time. But we're not supposed to go blabbing it around. They said most people wouldn't believe me so why ask for trouble, they said."

I told Dave that I appreciated the faith and trust he had placed in me, and by then I was feeling a bit guilty about some of the thoughts about him that had crossed my mind as he'd related his story over the hours.

I did not seek Dave's permission to use his story in this book. However, I have taken every precaution to protect his anonymity so as not to violate his trust. I have simply related a tale, true or not, and have not exposed him to the possibility of any public ridicule.

We shook hands and said goodbye on the sidewalk near the entrance to the train station and he headed off to catch his ride. I then spotted Paul in full incarnate form, still dressed in the suit and carrying the briefcase, walking toward me. He and Dave passed one another close enough to touch. Paul, in his inimitable teasing style, smiled and said "good afternoon" to Dave, who remained oblivious to the greeting. Perhaps he didn't hear it, but I did. I knew that the gesture was for my benefit—my entertainment, actually. It was a typical Paul shenanigan.

Pedestrians sidestepped Paul, as he did them, so I knew that he was truly visible this time for the whole world to see. But he was just another guy on the streets of the big city, and what more fitting city to be in than the City of Angels?

"What do you make of that?" I asked as we started walking again. "Do you think that story is true? It sounds crazy to me, but Dave doesn't seem crazy. He's not highly educated, and he's probably a bit naive, but he seems sane enough.

Do you think Marco is really a hybrid?"

I guess I should have given Paul a chance to respond, but the questions just came pouring out of me. We cut over to Broadway and headed toward the *Times* building again. I was feeling invigorated from the exercise and just being outdoors in the bustle and excitement of the city on a splendid day.

"It's a very large universe," Paul replied. "There's room for some mighty strange things. In fact, I suspect that your most outrageous and extreme fantasy could never equal the reality of what exists out there. It ranges from the stunningly beautiful to the abominably grotesque, and everything in between. As for whether Dave's story about Marco is true, I leave that to you decide."

"I thought you would find the idea of such tinkering with nature abhorrent," I said. "Aren't you offended? I must admit that even I, a non-religious person, would find the practice slightly disturbing if it turned out to be a fact. If this is really being done, I would like to know why," I said. "What possible reason could there be and what purposes would be served?"

Paul said that if indeed such practices were going on—and he would neither confirm nor deny whether he had any knowledge of the subject—he suspected that the answer would be phrased in lofty scientific, psychological, and social terms, but what it would really come down to was "because they could." Just as plant life has been cross-pollinated and animals cross-bred for a long time here on Earth, the adherents of a Star Seed program most likely would claim that such a program is geared toward improvement of the species.

Eventually the conversation got around once again to previous discussions that we had had concerning the complex and convoluted hidden dynamics of my extended family specifically and the typical family in general. Despite the stereotype of the harmonious TV family of the 1950s, I believe that the average family—American and otherwise—is rife with discord.

"What did I tell you at that time? I told you to remember the conversation because there was an important message there—that is, people are not always who they say or believe they are, and rarely are they what others think they are."

"I will concede that you did say that," I said with mock stiff formality.

"Good. Okay, Marco is a prime example of that very message. Remember also when we first began meeting that I told you that you would get a chance to develop and hone your telepathic skills?"

"I also concede that point," I acknowledged in the same manner. "You said most people have the inherent ability but that few ever discover it, let alone use it."

I don't know why I was being so flippant with my responses. Perhaps the reason for it was the stress of the hours-long conversation with Dave during which I felt compelled to maintain a serious, if not somber, expression.

In any case, Paul didn't respond to my attempt at levity. He said that he wanted me to begin experimenting with trying to send and receive telepathic messages. I put aside my juvenile attitude and settled down, at which time something else suddenly registered on my brain: Paul had just talked about Marco as though he knew him! I immediately grilled him on that point and he admitted that he had made "certain arrangements" for me to run into Dave and Marco at the train station.

"You set it up?" I asked.

"I arranged for you to be there and hoped that Dave would spot you. I didn't directly contact him or the boy, no. They don't know I exist. To tell you the truth, I had tried several times in the past to put the three of you in contact, but something happened each time to keep the meeting from occurring. You kept missing each other by seconds. This time, it finally worked. Dave spotted you, he had Marco with him, and your personalities just did what comes naturally."

"You know," I said to Paul at one point on our walk, "it's pretty obvious that we are not off on a random adventure or just engaging in idle chatter. My instincts tell me that a lot of things we have talked about today have had a purpose."

"It's that manifest, is it?" he said with a grin.

Sometimes it takes me a second or two to catch on to his teasing.

"Well, you are right. And I commend you on your discernment," he continued.

Now I wondered if he was turning the tables and being frivolous with me. Whatever. He continued in a serious vein.

"Marco is an extraordinary boy with a great gift. He is a natural telepath. I wanted you to meet him because he will be your unwitting mentor as you attempt to develop your own latent telepathic abilities."

"Then he is a Star Child?" I asked in amazement.

"I didn't say that. I told you before that you will have to decide that for yourself. That has nothing to do with me," he said

Had I annoyed him? Can angels become testy?

"Whether I approve or disapprove of any interspecies experimentation is not relevant," Paul went on. "The only thing that matters to me is that he was created and is alive. He had no choice in the matter of being born and I would never judge him on the basis of the circumstances of his conception or birth, nor anyone else for that matter. So we will not discuss the subject of his genealogy."

So that was it! I guessed that there was a moral issue involved with Paul. At least that's the message I was getting.

I felt like a stooge, a bonehead. I should have seen the indications and kept my mouth shut. This was an extremely sensitive subject to him; I dropped it immediately. I personally don't have any moral, ethical, spiritual, philosophical, or any other kind of objections to interspecies experimentation to produce hybrid children as long as there is sound science behind it. That is, I would expect that the scientific researchers would have done the necessary groundwork and taken the required precautions to ensure that the resultant children would be, at the minimum, genetically equal to—and preferably superior to—both parents.

But as far as I was concerned, this was all theoretical anyway because I had not yet accepted as fact that such hybrid children did indeed exist, or even that any attempt at interspecies breeding had been attempted. Marco was certainly a most unusual boy, but that didn't prove anything. If indeed such hybridization experiments were being conducted, I could understand why Paul might not approve on a spiritual level. I couldn't say for sure that he actually disapproved—he merely said that he didn't want to discuss the issue. Well, I wouldn't bring it up again.

Our random wandering found us back at a corner of the *Times* building at Broadway and First Street. It was mid-afternoon and a trickle of people began coming out of the buildings with the start of the evening commuter rush. The streets were beginning to get more crowded with pedestrians and vehicles. It had been several years since I last visited the newspaper, not counting this day's earlier visit, naturally. We walked slowly around the entire complex. We didn't say much during that time and Paul was perceptive enough to sense my mood and not intrude.

After circling the block, we headed north on Spring Street back toward Union Station.

During the train ride back to my home Paul described for me some relaxation techniques to use when I decided to attempt to develop my telepathic skills. Because Marco had met me, had touched me, and had spoken to me, he had become attuned to my existence. That was not necessarily a prerequisite for communication, Paul explained, but it could be considered a form of reinforcement for Marco to be receptive to my thought transmissions. It was now up to me to work on sending and receiving clear communications. That would take practice, practice, practice, and even then there was no guarantee of the level of success that I might achieve, if any, Paul said. He did concede, however, that I was a good candidate and that he expected me to develop a reasonable degree of proficiency if I really applied myself.

He instructed me on how to clear my mind, how to open channels, as it were, for the information to flow, and then how to direct my thoughts to the person I was trying to contact. There is no real mystery to the process. I suppose people who meditate—I am not one of them—are pretty good at clearing their minds. Relaxation is probably the most important element and the techniques for achieving it are pretty common. The basic idea is to focus the mind first on the physical body, beginning at the extremities and working one's way up the body to the top of the head.

When one is tightly focused on, say, getting the toes or the calf muscles or the thighs to relax, the mind becomes cleared of all extraneousness. Thoughts of work, relationships, politics, religion, the news—whatever one normally thinks about during the course of the day—are expunged like so many toxins. After one has gone through all the major muscle groups of the body and it has totally relaxed—which it will if the exercise is successful—the mind goes into a state of emptiness that is, paradoxically, acutely aware.

Most of the further instructions included mental exercises. But until I achieved some moderate degree of success, if I ever did, Paul suggested I should concentrate almost exclusively on trying to open up a psychic connection with Marco.

"What did you mean by an 'unwitting' mentor?" I asked. "Does that mean Marco has not been consulted?"

"He has not been approached by anyone on your behalf, but because he is such a highly accomplished telepath, he would be a good one to try to establish contact with. Expert telepaths have an unwritten code that encourages them to help novices from whom they pick up communications, no matter how rudimentary," Paul said. "So, if you do succeed in sending a communication that is received by Marco, he will take an interest in you and try to help you develop your technique. Of that I am certain."

This was heady stuff, even for a believer. But for someone who only a few years earlier considered such ideas, practices, and beliefs as sheer lunacy, it was more than heady—it was miraculous. We're talking about phenomena so far outside the realm of my own previous conventional thought processes that it could blow my head right off my shoulders if I didn't work at keeping my perspective.

I mostly stared out the window on the ride home, not seeing much. Paul seemed to have the ability to read me quite well, though. He was probably aware of my mood at the time as well as the hodge-podge of emotions and sweeping thoughts that were racing around inside my brain, and yet he was gracious enough not to make any attempt to intrude. If I had to describe my mental state in one word, I suppose I would have to call it philosophical. Or was it just dreamy? I certainly was not going to be able to come to grips with this new reality during a forty-five-minute train ride, and so Paul left me to myself for nearly a week.

I became more or less secluded in my office/den for that period, thinking, reminiscing, writing down my thoughts, and annotating recent events. I needed that time as desperately as I needed the air in the room. Finally, when I emerged six days later, renewed, relaxed, and reconciled to my new reality, Paul was waiting for me. After seeing my wife off to work, drinking a cup of hot green tea and reading the morning paper, I stepped out of the house after nearly a week of indoor isolation, hopped onto my mountain bike, and headed out into the sunshine and fresh air.

It's a pleasant ride to the bike trail that snakes for miles along the valley floor, mostly because the two-mile journey to get there is almost all downhill and I hardly have to break a sweat doing any pedaling. I barely got onto the trail before Paul came barreling out of one of the neighborhood entrances and fell in beside me on a very ordinary looking ten-speed bike. I remember wondering at the time where he got his props—not just the bike, but his clothing as well. And that briefcase had been quite a touch. Were they real? An illusion? An apparition like him? It was just a momentary thought, however, and I soon forgot about it as we began discussing more important matters.

"You're looking good," he said cheerfully.

I was working pretty hard on the pedals but Paul seemed to exert no effort at all as he coasted along beside me.

"Feeling pretty good, too," I replied. "Got a lot of things sorted out in my mind, but I've got a bag of questions that need to be answered to fill in some of the gaps."

"I knew you would. That's why I'm here. I've been waiting for you to come out of your cocoon," he said. "I can talk and ride at the same time, but I think it would be a lot easier on you if we made a pit stop."

He was right, as usual. We were tearing along at a pretty good clip and we had already covered close to half a mile.

While I was working up a sweat pumping away at a strenuous pace, Paul was going through the motions of pedaling, but it was obvious that he wasn't doing any work at all. He looked as relaxed as though he were lying in a hammock somewhere sipping a glass of lemonade, while I was working at near capacity just to stay even with him. We pulled off the trail and brought our bikes to a halt. A gravel equestrian and pedestrian track parallels the paved bike trail, but both courses were virtually empty, with only an occasional jogger or bicyclist passing by as we talked.

"I've come to grips with what you told me," I began. "I've been spending a lot of time trying to make telepathic contact with Marco. I don't seem to be getting anywhere. Maybe I'm not suited for that sort of thing. I guess it wouldn't be any big deal if I failed, but the idea sure is exciting and compelling."

"Do you want it to work?"

"Oh, sure. I think it would be great. But I'm also a realist—and a skeptic, as well, as you know—and I'm not pinning any great hopes on being successful. If it works, great. If it doesn't, well that's life."

"It won't work with that attitude," Paul said. "I should have told you. You have to believe."

"You know that I'm not a man of faith," I said.

"I'm not talking about faith. I'm talking about self-confidence."

We batted the subject around for a while, with me mostly on the defensive as I put up puny arguments to each of Paul's points. He knocked them all down until I finally admitted that perhaps I did have a bit of a defeatist attitude in this area and may not have expected to succeed. Paul said I would have to work on clearing my mind of negative thoughts and endeavor to adopt a positive attitude when I went into telepathic mode. I vowed to continue trying.

We walked our bicycles for a bit, then stopped again and stretched out on the ground off to the side. I couldn't get comfortable sitting on the ground, so I squirmed through several positions. I sat with my arms folded around my bent knees. I rested in a prone position with an elbow on the ground, my head cradled in a hand. Finally I gave up and got to my feet and found a comfortable position leaning on the bike.

"Sometimes I think I'm a Star Child," I told Paul whimsically.

"Believe me, you're not," he said, laughing heartily.

"Yeah, if the theoretical purpose is to improve the fruit of the family tree, I think I would be considered a lemon," I continued.

We both laughed. I come from average people, so if I were one of these theoretical children with an extraterrestrial father, unless he was a bit slower in brainpower relative to the human race, I don't think I would represent any improvement over either breed. While I was being glibly self-deprecating, it would have been nice if Paul had protested even slightly and told me that I was being too hard on myself. I almost winced when he agreed after I mentioned that I had lived a virtually unspectacular life, had made no notable contributions to society beyond what is expected of the average person (obeying the law, respecting others, paying one's taxes, etc.), and had never risen to any position of prominence among my fellow humans other than through the few books I had written.

However, he reminded me that I had not yet croaked and repeated the assertion that "important work" for me still lay ahead. I was getting a little tired of hearing that phrase, especially when no explanation was provided. I was raised in a small blue-collar town at a time when few women worked outside of the household. These were the years of the Great

Depression and later a world war, when the country was going through some mighty hard times, before the emergence of a large middle class. The majority of American families struggled, and poverty was rampant.

It is also important to understand the circumstances of the average working-class family at the time. It was typically too large, crowded into a too-small house, the parents weary and beaten down by the daily struggle for existence. There was also an underlying culture of class consciousness, an acceptance of one's station in life as almost inevitable. If they ever thought about the future, their mind-set was that the girls would get married and the boys would go to work. College wasn't even a consideration; nobody in their families went to college, as college was for the privileged and lucky few.

"It's true that you haven't exactly been an over-achiever, but you have survived," Paul said. "That in itself is some sort of achievement. Tell me honestly, didn't you ever feel different when you were growing up?"

"Different than what?"

"Different from others around you. Didn't you ever feel set apart?"

"You mean left out? Not at all. I was a luminary among the high-school in-crowd, a virtual VIP. Popular was my middle name."

"I see," he said dryly.

"Sorry," I said with a smirk and a chuckle. "Okay, so I wasn't prom king. Back to your question. Did I feel left out, you asked?"

"Well, that too. But I was thinking more along the line of feeling that others—childhood peers and adults alike—didn't really understand you at times."

I suppose I did, sometimes. I knew that others thought I was stupid, and I was often in concurrence. And why not?

My lack of interest in school and my grades proved that. When parents are too busy dealing with the hardships of life, they often don't have the energy or time to supervise their children adequately, including taking an interest in their education.

The only interest I seemed to have had was pursuing those activities that proved so alluring to such all-American boys as Tom Sawyer and Huck Finn. I never gave much thought to anything beyond the immediate day and what adventures it might hold. I made time for school and homework only when I couldn't avoid it. They were just an intrusion into which I put the minimum effort just to get by.

The fact is, now that I look back upon my childhood from the perspective of a fairly well-balanced, mature adult, if I were that same schoolboy today I probably would be on Ritalin or some other drug to treat Attention Deficit Hyperactivity Disorder (ADHD).

Despite my lackluster educational credentials, I did read a lot. I read comic books, catalogues, newspapers, old magazines. I even occasionally read my textbooks. I read the dictionary and the *World Book Encyclopedia*. I read the backs of cereal boxes and I read the stacks of dog-eared, hand-me-down penny dreadfuls and paperbacks that my parents had picked up here and there. I also had a library card.

Every so often I got this strange notion that I was capable of doing better than my report cards indicated. This feeling was reinforced when one day, in a tenth-grade English class, the teacher—yes, the same teacher who possessed such an intimate knowledge and understanding of the mysteries of the universe—began to read aloud an essay assignment on comic books that I had written.

Four or five paragraphs into it, she stopped and, with a dramatic flourish, ripped it in half and tossed it into the wastepaper basket.

"This was copied," she proclaimed.

I was mortified. I liked comic books, and I had read some reference material on them, primarily from the encyclopedia, before writing my essay. I suppose it was a compliment in a way because she mistook my writing for a job beyond the ability of an average tenth-grader, or at least for this tenth-grader whose classroom work didn't appear to indicate any hidden potential. At that moment, I thought that if I was dumb, this jerk teacher was even dumber. Nevertheless, it was a painful experience.

"I remember the incident quite well," Paul told me.

"That's right," I said, suddenly realizing that he likely had been there with me. "You could have helped me out a bit there," I said, feigning a pout.

"It didn't kill you," he replied.

"How come I couldn't have been born into a rich family? Or at least one where they would have taken a hickory stick to me when I didn't study or got bad grades?" I asked puckishly.

"Oh, come on now," Paul said, "you got through it okay. Besides, I think you should have seen the signs a long time ago, even if it wasn't during your childhood, that something unusual was going on."

For the next half hour, Paul cited a host of incidents spanning childhood through young adulthood that, when toted up, should have tipped me off that I was either extremely lucky or blessed in some way as I made my way through life. Still, it never would have occurred to me that I had a guardian angel looking after me. And yet here I was, face-to-face with that angel—an encounter that I would have previously considered beyond the fathomable.

I must have been a real handful, I told Paul. Memories were revived as he talked. For example, he reminded me of an experience I had as a young soldier shortly after I was drafted in 1954.

I was sitting in a dusty field with the rest of my company eating midday chow that included beef stew. Basic training was grueling, and while the army provided the proper number of calories to sustain a body, our mothers weren't there to bring us milk and cookies (not that mine ever did). Recruits didn't have the luxury of going to the refrigerator for a snack anytime they felt like it, and so we were always hungry. Ergo, we didn't waste food, precious calories that our changing bodies were always pestering us for as we shed fat and built muscle.

I was gnawing away at a particularly gristly chunk of stew meat that could easily have substituted for the leather in the boots I was wearing. I had a set of good, strong 19-year-old teeth—well, I was 19; I guess my teeth would have been about 10 or 11—but even those were no match for this piece of rubbery gristle. I couldn't bite through it and yet my hunger wouldn't let me spit it out, so I tried to swallow it whole. It lodged in my throat. I made a couple of futile gulps to try to force it down. When that failed, I tried to cough it up. It was wedged securely.

I couldn't breathe, so I did the only logical thing that would occur to a kid of nineteen who had not yet tasted life and who wanted to keep breathing for a while—I panicked. I jumped up and ran mindlessly in a blind frenzy, drawing a stream of curses and shouts from the other soldiers into whose mess kits I kicked a storm of dirt and dust as I raced among them. Dr. H.J. Heimlich was only thirty-three or thirty-four years old at the time and hadn't yet developed his maneuver for dislodging such obstructions. Those around me had no inkling as to what was occurring—at least I like to think so, considering that no one offered to help.

My burning lungs desperately and vainly tried sucking

for air and I knew that I had but a few seconds left before I slipped into unconsciousness. I would be dead within a few minutes, certainly before anyone realized what was happening and could help. I had run perhaps fifty or sixty yards in sheer terror, knowing that I was going to die. But then quite suddenly the obstruction was gone and I gasped in huge volumes of wonderful air. Afterward, I figured that the jarring that my body had taken from the panicked running had jolted the gristle loose and that I had swallowed it. I know I didn't inhale it or cough it up.

"You do keep a protector busy at times," Paul said whimsically. "I'm not sure the Heimlich maneuver would have worked even if it had been available. That thing was really stuck in there," he said.

"Well, it's never too late to say thanks," I said, "so, thanks. I appreciate it."

Once I returned to civilian life, and didn't have to worry daily about starving, I more or less gave up meat.

"Think it could have been a delayed reaction to that experience?" I asked.

"Perhaps," Paul replied. "Practice your telepathy."

With that, he rode off effortlessly on his bike. I faced the prospect of the mostly uphill return trip to my house.

Observation By Paul

"It is absolutely vital that some children
be seen and heard, not the opposite,
for they can remind us of what we once
knew, but have since forgotten,
when we were their age."

testing paul

When time for my family reunion came around, I wasn't really interested in attending. But my wife, of all people, thought it would be an adventure, so I relented and finally agreed to go. Although I had been back to my hometown for brief periods of several days, I had merely passed through after stopping to see my parents and a relative or two. This was to be a more intense visit.

Even after I learned about Paul, I never took unnecessary risks with the thought that he would always be there to pull me out of any tight spots that I recklessly got myself into. I practiced what I preached to the New York cabby—stop at all red traffic signals. But there was one exception that occurred in June of 2002.

It began when my wife and I flew into Providence, Rhode Island (I spotted Paul on the flight, naturally), toured a bit in New England, visited a friend in Connecticut, then headed down to my hometown. The summer weather was typical Pennsylvania—muggy. The main drag runs through the center of town along the bottom of the glen in which the town sits, with the residential neighborhoods rising into the low hills on either side. The town is only about a mile long and no part of it is more than five minutes away by car.

The reunion was uneventful, and my wife enjoyed meeting and socializing with many newfound friends and several people whom she had met briefly on previous visits. I was surprised that I recognized a number of people I hadn't seen in five decades. There were a few I didn't recognize because of the changes that had taken place over time. There were also those who were complete strangers to me, born after I had gone off to California.

Afterward, I talked my wife into going with me to a nearby town to visit an old childhood buddy named Mel. We had rediscovered one another on the Internet several years earlier and had exchanged addresses and phone numbers.

Mel and I had been frequent and easy targets for all of the bullies from elementary school through high school, although I did escape during the first few days of the twelfth grade when I left town for good, hauled off to California by my parents. However, I hadn't really escaped, but merely changed tormentors. The only difference was that the California bullies were more tanned and didn't have much opportunity to shove fistfuls of snow down my back.

Mel and I had lived in separate but nearby towns as kids and attended different schools. We had met through a cousin of mine and became fast friends, one reason being that we shared a common activity during our leisure time—the enjoyment of being tyrannized by troglodytes for years while still maintaining a fairly cheery outlook on life in general. We usually saw each other on weekends a dozen or so times a year and traded stories about our various adventures of victimhood.

What really had tightened the bonds was the fact that

we were both so puny that even glandular freaks from classes behind us joined in the fun. That is, some kids younger than us and in lower classes also targeted us for wedgies, Indian rubs, pantsing—yanking the victim's trousers down in public (in front of girls, of course, for maximum effect)—and all of the other forms of entertainment enjoyed by high-spirited adolescents.

Mel had stayed in the area, married a girl from his church, had several grown children, and owned a modest home that was free and clear. Although I was fortunate to have taken early retirement nine years earlier, Mel was still working here and there, although he had left his full-time job and was collecting Social Security. I didn't ask, but I presumed that he worked to remain active rather than out of financial necessity.

He had changed, of course, but I still recognized him. It's a strange phenomenon to see someone after decades of separation. The mind's eye holds a picture of what the person looked like as a kid, which is in sharp contrast to the current reality. It's like an instant transformation, going from being a kid to an old man in one fell swoop. The brain reels momentarily, trying to reconcile the old memory with the new reality.

Mel was still small, and although I am not a big man I had managed to stretch out to about five feet ten or eleven inches and pack on enough weight to tip the scales at 170 pounds, which made me larger than Mel. I also had managed to keep most of my hair.

I had called ahead, so he was expecting me, waiting in the driveway with his wife when my wife and I drove up to his house. I didn't initiate it, but the embrace didn't make me feel too uneasy when he caught me in a big bear hug almost before I could get out of the car. We were genuinely glad to see each other after all these years. We introduced our spouses, toured his house, and drank iced tea and talked about old times for several hours.

Mel gave up on the iced tea pretty quickly and began swigging from bottles of beer. I declined his offer and stuck with the tea. It wasn't long before the beer had flushed out some ancient memories that floated around loosely in Mel's head and began pouring out of his mouth.

"You know, this old boy nearly ripped his arm off one summer," Mel said to his wife, Kathy, "when he fell out of a tree. 'Member that?" Mel asked, the alcohol starting to show in the elided words that began to tumble clumsily from his tongue.

I remembered, all right. My guardian angel and I had discussed the incident thoroughly during one of several conversations in which Paul had responded to my inquiries about the number of times he had come to my aid. It was the first day of summer vacation from school, a Saturday in June of maybe 1946, when I was about eleven years old. I was supposed to be doing my Saturday housecleaning chores but had slipped out of the house to join a group of pals who were off on some adventure.

It was impossible for me to stay home and vacuum and make beds on a beckoning sunny Saturday morning when my buddies were headed up to the woods behind our block for who-knows-what-kind of unimaginable exploits. So off we went, about half a dozen of us, whooping, shoving, leaping, dashing hither and thither, moving as a single amorphous unit toward our objective. The woods ran along the southeast edge of the town and all it took was a quick, trespassing dash through a neighbor's yard to reach them. There was also the option of walking to the cross streets on either end of the block to gain access, but I don't believe that was ever given any consideration.

I must have spent half of my childhood in those woods,

and half of that time was spent twenty feet off the ground in the branches of the trees. Every superhero ever immortalized in a comic book or a movie serial had populated these woods at one time or another. Tarzan had swung from tree to tree on vines that carried him through the forest faster than any lion could sprint. Batman and Robin, Superman and Captain America had made numerous heroic dashes, capes flying, through the woods on some crime-fighting mission or another. Secret hiding places abounded, and there was an unofficial clubhouse jerry-rigged together out of scrap wood built over a hole dug into the forest floor.

To make it easier to scale some of the thinner trees with flimsy branches that were mostly out of reach from the ground, we had taken to hammering large, heavy construction spikes into the trees for foot- and hand-holds to allow us to scale the trees. At the moment in question, I was about fifteen or twenty feet above the ground—at least that's the way I remember it from a small kid's perspective—in one of those very trees when the gang decided to move on deeper into the woods. I didn't want to be left behind, and in my haste to climb down I missed one of the nails with my foot. I plunged to the ground, upright and parallel to the tree, arms outstretched above my head. I was small and lightweight and didn't build up much kinetic energy in a fall onto soft, leaf-covered Earth, landing feet-first and not even crumbling to the ground.

I was unhurt. Or so I thought until I discovered a nasty scrape on the inside of my right arm, running from the wrist to the biceps where it disappeared under the sleeve of my shirt. It started to burn. I pushed the sleeve up to keep from getting blood on it and my thumb sank into a bloody, ragged hole in my biceps. I stared in shock at the jagged tear momentarily and saw the main artery in the arm pulsating. It had been exposed but not torn. It seemed that half of the muscle was gone, and when

I turned my attention back to the tree I saw a mass of bloody flesh hanging from one of the spikes about ten feet up the tree.

I let out a yelp of horror and sped for home, followed by the other boys. I dashed into the house and showed the gaping wound to my mother in the upstairs bathroom where she was finishing the chores that I was supposed to be doing. She turned white, then looked out the window and saw that Doc Weaver's car was parked in his garage in the alley below and behind our row of houses, and quickly sent me off to him.

Doc Weaver was the town miracle worker who tended to any ailment known to befall humans. He dried my tears, calmed me down, stitched my wound closed, bandaged me up, and sent me on my way, all done with a quiet, methodical, soothing proficiency. I like to think that my parents paid him at some point for his services. Probably not, though.

I wasn't expecting any medals when I got home, but neither was I expecting to be subjected to one of my father's fearsome outbursts. He had been summoned by one of my brothers from his place of work nearby.

"See what you've done to your mother!" he bellowed as he cuddled his sobbing wife in his arms.

Yeah, my poor mom. How could I have been so inconsiderate? I spent the next few days confined to my bed. In our house, one didn't get sent to one's room, one got sent to bed, mainly because one didn't have a room of his own—nor an unshared bed, for that matter.

It wasn't until decades later that I would learn that Paul had been at my side, and while he did not prevent the fall or the nasty cut, he did manage to pull my head back just enough to keep one of the spikes in the tree from catching me under the chin and possibly ripping out my jugular vein. At least that's what he implies, and I have no reason to disbelieve him. I know that I wasn't the fastest runner among the group of boys who witnessed my fall, but when we all stampeded toward my house, my feet suddenly acquired the wings of Mercury and I left even the fleetest among the group eating my dust.

I turned my attention back to Mel, who had cracked open another beer, probably his third or fourth by now.

"Hey, I have an idea," Mel said. "Let's go to a tavern and have a little party."

He was feeling no pain at that point. My wife declined, and that gave Mel's wife an excuse to also beg off; the mere mention of going to the tavern seemed to cause a spasm of pain to rake across her face. I hadn't known Kathy as a kid. She was several grades behind Mel and was from his hometown. She looked like she probably was pretty, or at least cute, when she was younger, but time had blunted the features, grayed the hair, wrinkled the skin, and most likely had added a bit of weight to her fairly ample frame. She wasn't as tall as Mel, but I would have bet that she outweighed him by 20 or 30 pounds.

I tried not to speculate on what the dullness in her eyes or the look of pain on her face at the mention of the tavern said about their private life. It was obvious though that she was relieved when my wife said she wasn't interested in going along. Kathy fairly bubbled with enthusiasm and offered to make some hot tea, suggesting that they would have a nice chat while we guys were out boozing.

It was only after some resistance from Mel that I was able to talk him into letting me drive. The towns in Pennsylvania have an interesting feature that may or may not be unique to the state. That is, neighborhood beer bars are scattered throughout residential sections. Some of the homes actually have been converted to drinking establishments, with the bar in the parlor area and the rest of the house used as a residence.

Mel guided me as I drove and we arrived at one of his favorite watering holes. There were two other people in the bar when we entered, besides the bartender. At the end of the bar sat a toothless old guy who looked to be seventy-five, gazing into his glass of beer with his chin resting on his forearms that were folded onto the bar. A cigarette smoldered forgotten in the full ashtray in front of him and another dangled out of the corner of his mouth.

The other was a large, beefy man also puffing on a cigarette with a full ashtray of stubs in front of him beside his glass of beer. Even though he looked to be mid-to-late 60s, he also looked tough and menacing as he gave us a long gaze up and down when we entered. He was wearing a sweat-stained blue work shirt with matching pants, and heavy work boots with white socks. Incongruously, he was holding a little mutt in his lap that was badly in need of some grooming of its matted coat.

"Jimmy, my man, where's it at?" Mel hollered at the bartender as we took seats.

"Hey, Mel, where you been hiding? Still doing that painting job? Where's Kathy? She let you out by yourself?"

"S'okay, I've got another designated driver tonight."

"Coupla brewskis?" Jimmy asked.

"Just a diet cola for me if you have one. Name's Phil," I added, reaching out a hand, which the bartender shook firmly.

"Finished the painting job yesterday," Mel said to Jimmy. "Know of any other work around? I'm free for the moment. Might have some excavation work for a septic tank coming up though."

Jimmy set the drinks down in front of us. Mel swilled half his glass of suds in one gulp. I guess it would have been too much to expect a straw in this place, but even a glass to go with my coke would have been a nice touch. I popped the top on the soda can and took a small swig.

I was sitting to Mel's right and the other two patrons were seated to his left. As I faced Mel for conversation, I noticed that the burly character a couple of seats away in the middle of the bar still had his eyes fixed on us while he absentmindedly petted the dog, which occasionally licked at some spilled beer on the bar and took a few laps from his owner's glass when it was offered.

Mel noticed me looking past him and turned to see what was grabbing my attention.

"Oh, hi, Eddie. How's it going? Kinda dark in here. I didn't recognize you at first," Mel said. He introduced me by name to the stranger.

The big man gave me the eye. He gulped down the remainder of his beer and raised the glass to the bartender, who brought him another one. He stubbed out his cigarette and immediately lit another. Jimmy took the full ashtray, dumped its contents into a receptacle under the bar, wiped it with the towel over his shoulder and replaced it. I noticed that the dog licked the big man's mouth every once in a while, and instead of flinching away in disgust, the owner almost seemed to return the "kiss." Maybe he had a tender side after all, even if it struck me as slightly repulsive.

I couldn't come up with a last name for the big guy, but there was something familiar about him even after all this time.

"This is Eddie Dwyer," Mel said. "You 'member Eddie, don't you?" he asked me. "We used to horse around together when we were kids."

Mel's mood had changed. He had gotten fidgety and I got the impression that he was being diffident—almost slavish—toward the big man, whose presence obviously was making him uncomfortable. This was mostly below the surface, with just a subtle ripple of disturbance.

Normally, I would have reached across Mel to offer the big man a hand, but there was something about him that told me to keep my distance. I simply nodded, said "hi," and kept racking my brain for some inkling of recognition, some piece of faded memory; there was indeed something vaguely familiar about the aged features, the name, but it proved too slippery for me to get my brain around.

"We knew each other as kids?" Eddie asked. "I don't remember you. You live around here?"

"California," I said. "Just visiting."

Eddie snorted and took another long draw on his beer. I noticed that it took him only two gulps to finish a full glass.

"Oh, the left coast. The land of fruits and nuts. You a fruit like your pal there?" Eddie asked.

Mel laughed nervously.

"C'mon, Eddie, you know I'm not a fruit. Neither is he."

Now Mel may be kind of wimpy, but he does have a sense of humor, which can emerge under even the most solemn occasion. He turned to look at me.

"You aren't, are you?" he asked wickedly.

If I had been taking a sip of my cola at the time it surely would have squirted out of my nose as I burst into a spasm of laughter. Maybe being kicked around so much encouraged him to develop a defense mechanism of levity to try to defuse potentially explosive situations. Anyone could see that the scowling big man didn't get the joke.

"Boy, that hit the spot. Well, we'd better get going," Mel said, throwing two or three dollar bills on the bar. He took a step or two toward the door and I started to swing off my seat to join him.

"What's your hurry?" Eddie demanded in a loud voice. "You two fairies going off to be alone?"

Now I was getting nervous. The guy was not only base and ignorant, he was drunk to boot, and no man talks to people that way—stranger or acquaintance—unless he's looking for trouble. He was, and I sure wasn't. And it was obvious that Mel wasn't. The bartender busied himself with polishing beer glasses and avoiding eye contact with any of us.

"No, we just stopped in for a minute," Mel said hesitantly. "Our wives are waiting for us. We're going out to dinner."

The mangy mutt continued to periodically lick Eddie's slobbering lips even as he told—actually commanded—Mel and me to sit down and have another beer with him.

"Well, okay, maybe just one more—but then we have to hit the road," Mel said, trying to control his voice and appear cheerful, but any halfway sober person could easily detect the nervousness in his manner and the stress in his voice, which almost cracked.

"Nothing else for me, thanks," I said, "but I'll sit for a while until Mel's ready."

"Give them both a beer," Eddie said to the bartender, who immediately drew two glasses of draft and set them in front of us. Mel picked up his, nudged me nervously with his elbow, turned to Eddie and raised the glass in his direction, saying, "Thanks, Eddie. Here's to you. Mighty generous of you."

I followed his example and raised my glass of beer toward the big man. Mel took a big gulp of his while I took a sip and placed the glass back on the bar. Eddie was preoccupied at the moment petting the mutt, baby-talking to it, and returning its kisses. Mel took the opportunity during the distraction to speak to me *sotto voce*.

"We gotta get outa here. I'll tell you about him later. He's trouble."

"Hell, don't thank me. I'm not buying your ... beers," Eddie said. "I just said to stay and have another with me.

ch 12   testing paul

Fact is, I'll even let you buy mine too on this round."

"Oh, sure," Mel said. He pulled out a bill and handed it to the bartender. It was embarrassing to see another person being so servile. I was now starting to get a little angry, although I kept it in check because even though Eddie was about my age, he was still a bruiser of a man, much larger than I.

The door to the bar opened just then and a man stuck his head inside and asked if anyone there was driving a car with Rhode Island license plates. I was just about to answer when I saw the man's face. I found it more amusing than surprising.

I replied that the car belonged to me. Paul asked if I could move it forward a little bit to allow him to maneuver his car out from behind. He said he was blocked in. I knew that was malarkey, of course. Paul didn't need to drive, and there was no car close to mine when I had parked earlier. I told Mel and Eddie that I'd be right back and stepped out into the humid darkness with Paul.

"My advice to you, young man [relatively speaking, I presume], is to vacate those premises unless you want a repeat of a lesson administered to you when you were a kid," Paul said.

He didn't offer the advice with any sense of urgency, nor did he appear frantic or concerned in any way. I had no idea what he was talking about, nor could I remember any particular lesson that he had in mind—especially one that old. We stepped away from the front of the tavern to blend into the shadows. There was no car parked behind my rental. The darkness seemed to swallow up Paul and I lost sight of him momentarily. However, he had only dematerialized and now hovered by my rental car as an apparition. Anyone coming from the bar would have seen no sign of him or his "car" that supposedly had been blocked in. The presumption would be that I had moved my car, and that he had left.

"I don't understand," I said. "What lesson? And if I learned it once, what's the problem with learning it again?"

"You don't remember him, do you?"

"Who? The big guy?"

"Yes. It's one of the hooligans who used to knock you—and Mel, as well as a few others—around when you were kids."

It started sounding familiar, but I still couldn't put my finger on the name.

"You hardly knew him by his real name," Paul said. "You guys used to call him Simple Simon, but not to his face."

"Oh, my gosh, that's Simple Simon?" I blurted. "I remember that jerk. And you're right, he was always picking on the smaller guys."

I had had numerous run-ins with him and at least one major altercation. When I was about fifteen or sixteen I had made a disparaging remark about him that was overheard by some little trollop who got her kicks out of stirring up trouble, and she passed on the word. Simple Simon eventually caught up with me out in the open. Normally, I would have tried to run away, but for some reason my resentment got the better of me and I stood up to him; I suppose it could have had something to do with the hormonal changes going on in my body at the time. I easily talked him out of battering me into a pulp then and there and got him to agree to meet me that evening at a location where teenagers hung out. We would then settle the matter man to man.

Mel and some of his friends that I hung out with thought I was crazy. But defiance was raging through my body and I was tired of caving in to the Neanderthals. I could have gotten my father or several of my brothers to step in on my behalf, but my pride precluded that; I had to fight my own battles.

Unfortunately, moral indignation doesn't pack much of a punch, and so I got the stuffing beaten out of me. There's an old adage that a good big man will beat a good little man every time. Simple Simon was big and I was small, and that was just a fact of life that I had to live with. A couple of dozen local kids witnessed the carnage as Simple Simon pounded me at will. Every once in a while, I got in a lucky shot that stung his face or an ear, and I did manage to bloody his lip a bit. But for every wild swing that I landed, he hammered me with three or four solid punches. Most of them landed on my torso rather than on my face, which kept me from getting cut up too badly. But even the ones that slammed into a shoulder or my rib-cage felt like a kick from a mule.

I was really hurting. Finally, after climbing back to my feet half a dozen times, only to be pummeled back down, I just lay on the ground gasping. My whole body hurt, one eye was already closing, blood was oozing from my nose and a gash on my lower lip. Simple Simon sauntered away victorious, followed by several of his cronies and most of the onlookers, while I licked my wounds. I was tended by Mel and several of his buddies, and a couple of neutral observers. But I also noticed that not one of the half-dozen or so girls who had witnessed my humiliating defeat stuck around to commiserate with me. They all went skipping off with the victory party.

The guys who stayed praised me for my bravery. But I wasn't sure what I had proved by my foolish act—probably nothing, because even though the bullying continued, I never fought back after that.

The memory passed before my eyes in a flash while I was talking with Paul.

"Let's get going," Paul said. "Get your buddy and go somewhere else, preferably home. He's drunk, you know."

I knew Mel was drunk. Humans have historically sought ways to achieve an altered state of consciousness through mind-altering compounds. Mel was Joe Six-Pack.

I had stood up to Eddie only that one time and now, given this second opportunity, I wasn't in the mood to tuck my tail between my legs and skulk off into the shadows. Admittedly, I took a battering for my principles, but I had defended them as best I could. I informed Paul of my intentions to stick around. That was my right as a free citizen.

"Besides," I said with a mischievous grin, "I don't have to worry now that I know you are at my side. I didn't know that when I was a kid. Besides that, just where were you back then when I was getting the tar whaled out of me?"

He scornfully ignored the question.

"Okay, I'm telling you frankly now that I'm not going to bail you out if you get into trouble in there. I've told you what you have to do. If you won't listen, I can't force you."

I turned abruptly and walked away, entering the tavern even as Paul was still rebuking me. I took a seat between Mel and Simple Simon, which left only one empty stool between me and the big man. I noticed that Mel had finished his beer and was now working on mine. He finished it off and ordered two more. I was just about to object that I didn't want one when I realized that he was buying it for Simple Simon, not for me. I gave the ape a real visual going-over now that I realized who he was. I suppose it was because I was now seeing him from my perspective as a man, rather than as a skinny kid; I was looking at him now with a lifetime of experience behind me. I still had the good sense to be nervous, but I wasn't cowering.

Besides, if Paul really didn't care what kind of trouble I got myself into, why was he standing inside the door watching? Even more, why did he feel he had to let me know he was there? He was in his apparition mode. I took comfort from his presence.

Simple Simon accepted his beer without a word of acknowledgement toward Mel. He was still preoccupied with that scruffy mutt and was still returning its occasional licks on the mouth.

"Say, Eddie," I said, turning my back on Mel to stare into the gorilla's eyes, "I notice that your repulsive mutt periodically licks its ass and then occasionally licks you on the mouth, which you don't seem to mind. Why don't you just lick the dog's ass directly and save yourself a step in the process?"

The words had spilled out of me before I even had given them any thought and were now hanging frozen in the air. The bartender and Mel reacted with looks of astonishment, and even the old geezer down at the end of the bar, who had been in another world inside his head during this whole time, took his chin off his arms and looked up with glazed interest.

Jimmy dropped a glass that he had been polishing, and Mel gave me a sharp poke in the ribs. The ape's face went even colder and harder, if that was possible. My guts were churning, but I remained resolute. Simple Simon finally found his tongue and the words came out in a raging slur.

"Whad 'id you say?" he demanded as he slid off the barstool.

Mel jumped from his own stool and quickly placed himself between Eddie and me. That struck me as surprisingly courageous.

"He was jus' jokin', Eddie. It was a joke. He's a big kidder. Listen, we gotta get goin'," he said to me. "We're really late; gonna get inta trouble with the ladies. Let's go," he said, grabbing me by the arm.

I stood my ground.

"Now I 'member you," Eddie said. "Wise ass with a smart mouth."

I doubted that he remembered me. It was a one-size-fits-all description that could have been applied to any number of people that he had clashed with.

"Yeah, that's me. I never seem to learn."

"Yeah, I r'ember. Wise guy. Big mouth. You must be suicidal or something, eh? Or maybe you're packing a gun. You got a gun?"

He shoved Mel aside like a bag of feathers. I was now about the same size that Eddie had been the last time he pounded me. If he had quit growing at that point and waited a few years for me to catch up to him, we would have been pretty evenly matched. Unfortunately for me, he had grown also, and he was a fairly big man, slightly over six feet and easily 230 to 250 pounds.

"No, I don't have a gun," I said. I didn't tell him that I wished I had, that it would have come in handy at the moment.

He came at me slothfully and unevenly. I had no trouble backing away from him.

"I'm not going to get into a barroom brawl," I told Eddie. "You want to fight me, let's do it right. Like old times. Outside. Private. Man to man. In the morning. You're drunk now."

The brute paused. He seemed to mellow out somewhat. I could see the wheels turning in his head. I don't remember his ever losing a fight, probably because he never picked on anyone of equal size, so he may have been recalling any one of hundreds of pleasing skirmishes of his youth.

I negotiated with him, talked him into a later rematch of our previous fight. Something about the challenge seemed to appeal to him. If he was even capable of feeling, I believe that he felt there was a certain nostalgic romanticism about it—he could relive his youth, when life was a delight and full of promise, when he was young, strong, virile, fearless, and hadn't yet been beaten down by it. Perhaps that idea filled one of the empty spaces in what I suspected was probably a pretty drab existence.

We agreed to meet the next day at eight a.m. in a secluded spot not too far out of town, the site of our last bloody encounter—the blood having been mostly mine. I wasn't familiar with the area any more but Eddie was. It would be a Sunday and things would be relatively quiet. In exchange, Eddie would agree to not mop up the floor of the bar with me right at the moment.

I started thinking that I should have listened to Paul. I was going to get my butt kicked again. I really hoped Paul was bluffing when he said he wouldn't intrude.

If he wasn't, I needed a plan, and one was coming to mind.

The sun rose on a fairly cool, partially cloudy morning and by the time eight a.m. rolled around there were about a dozen of us in the park-like area—Eddie, myself, Mel, Jimmy the bartender, the old coot at the end of the bar, who also brought his wife along, and maybe half a dozen others who had heard about the fight the way news travels in a small town.

A small circle formed as Eddie stripped off his windbreaker and tossed it on the ground, where I also placed my jacket, neatly folded. I also had with me a black plastic case, which I placed on the ground. I snapped the case open, and the onlookers pressed in to see two ceremonial tomahawks displayed in the wells of a foam-rubber insert. The hatchets bore carved Indian symbols and were decorated with colorful strips of what might have been dyed leather. The collection belonged to Mel.

"Take your pick, Eddie," I said as I thrust the case in his direction.

A look of bewilderment played across his face. He seemed unable to comprehend the situation, so he merely stared dumbly, first at the tomahawks, then at me, then at the onlookers, then back at the war hatchets again.

"You took something from me," I said. "I'm here to take

it back. But the rules have changed. We fought on your terms before. Now we fight on mine."

Well, Eddie stepped in with every intention of busting me a good one in the mug, but thought better of it and took two steps back when I deftly armed myself with one of the weapons. Suddenly, the odds had evened out. Eddie was twice my size, but a blow from a keenly honed iron blade with some heft behind it, even delivered by a small man, could do some mighty mean damage. Simple Simon was enraged as I taunted him to take the remaining hatchet, and he nearly did half a dozen times, but always pulled back at the last moment. He knew that I was more nimble, quicker—and his size no longer was an advantage; it was actually a disadvantage.

As we circled, my eyes took in the small gathering, and right in the middle was Paul in full corporeal form, it appeared, dressed as casually as the locals in faded blue jeans and a rustic plaid shirt. He wore a look of detachment, but I wasn't fooled. He was with me.

"Come on Eddie, let's get to it," I taunted as I tracked him while he circled slowly, trying to keep his distance from me and the tomahawk clutched in my right hand. The case with the remaining blade lay on the ground, an open invitation to him.

"You're crazy," Eddie growled. "Fight like a man!" He wanted to smash me—a puny little squirt who was ridiculing him. But I could tell that he was thinking, probably about the pain of one blow from that blade digging into his rib cage, slicing through his neck, or splitting open his skull. Of course, he could do the same damage to me, if he was lucky. But he didn't like the odds.

"Do you know what we do in California?" I asked. "We jog. We run. We exercise. We stay fit. At least a lot of us do. California people practically live outdoors."

He was a lumbering clown, rolls of fat ringing his midsection, thick jowls fit for a prize porker, waddles that would make any turkey proud. He was an out-of shape old man now. It must have been quite a comedown.

He was puffing as we circled each other, with him looking for one opening—just one good opening—to club me with one of his massive fists. If he had found it, it would have been curtains for me. But he just wasn't fast enough. Four times I quickly shifted the weapon to my right hand and caught him flat-footed. I was in a good position to take a poke at him if I had wanted to.

Instead, on one of those four occasions I merely gave him my specialty—a fillip, a flick of the finger on the tip of his nose. I was not losing this battle, but there is a certain dubious honor even for the loser in a fistfight: The bloody and/or broken nose, the puffed lip, the cut on the cheek, the puffy eye, all marks of manliness in fighting circles. And there is nothing macho about being disdainfully flicked on the nose as though you were as insignificant as a mere gnat. I was now taking that away from Eddie also—the machismo. I was emasculating a once-proud, physically powerful human being, psychologically castrating him. This was unfinished business that finally was being dealt with.

But he refused to pick up the hatchet that reposed in the case on the ground. He knew that if he did, the confrontation could take on a most deadly turn, especially if I were as crazy as he suspected. If I was capable of moving in, flicking his nose with the snap of a finger and then moving out of range before he could react, then I would be able to chop him to pieces if we got into a serious battle with the weapons. Without a gun, he was defenseless.

I fervently hoped that he wouldn't go for the weapon in one insane moment.

You see, I was bluffing.

There was no way that I could have brought myself to hit him with the deadly blade. I simply would have had to concede by turning tail and getting my carcass out of there. More than once I caught sight of Paul leaning against a tree just beyond the small group of onlookers. He didn't look pleased, but then he didn't control my life either. Ultimately, at the moment, I was the master of my own destiny.

Finally, after about ten minutes, confused, angry, and dispirited, Simple Simon turned his back on me, pushed his way through the small crowd, and walked away, leaving behind not only his windbreaker but part of himself, which lay broken on the ground. I packed up the case, along with what I considered my reclaimed dignity and self-respect, put on my jacket and strode out of the clearing in the woods with Mel practically slobbering all over me. I handed him the case with the tomahawks.

"Thanks for the loan," I said. "They came in real handy."

"Oh, man, oh, man, you really destroyed him," Mel chimed gleefully. "That was so sweet. I've wanted to kill him for fifty years. And you did it. You killed him."

"He'll survive," I said. "I just changed the rules."

Observation By Paul

"There is a world of difference between a kiss and a bite, and the same messenger can deliver one as easily as the other."

opening communication

Paul was not happy with me, no doubt. I got that idea when I didn't see him again for about a month after I left him standing outside the tavern. After my showdown with Eddie, my wife and I did some sightseeing for about a week and then headed to Providence to catch our flight back home. If Paul was aboard, he didn't show himself, probably giving me the silent treatment.

Just when I thought that he had dropped out of my life, perhaps forever—at least on a visual level—he reappeared about a month later, on a dazzling August day, as I was taking a walk/jog through a magnificent public park in Northglenn, Colorado, just outside of Denver. I presume he had been on the flight with me as well, but I hadn't seen him. The meandering pedestrian path circled a man-made lake and probably was a good half-mile around. Paul fell in beside me after coming up from behind. I had just completed a leg of jogging and had settled back to a brisk walk. He was dressed for the part: T-shirt, shorts, athletic socks, and running shoes.

"What you did was immature, foolhardy, risky, and most likely illegal," he said abruptly, as though no time had passed between then and our last conversation.

"Good morning to you, too," I said cheerfully with a huge smile as perspiration ran off my brow. The weather was energizing, the setting spectacular, the park uncrowded, and my spirits were high. How could anyone be in a bad mood on such a glorious day? I was in town for four or five days to attend a conference at which I would be speaking.

"You can't count on me to come to your rescue every time you get into trouble," he said, "and that's especially true if you deliberately put yourself in peril under the false assumption that no harm can come to you just because I happen to be watching over you. People have guardian angels, but people also get hurt, they get sick, they get killed. You should know that I would not have protected you or come to your rescue in that fight. It was absolutely unnecessary and represented a huge error in judgment."

Wow. If he were just another guy, the words would have indicated without a doubt that the speaker was upset, angry, and frustrated. But the words carried no emotion. They were just information with no more passion than the data spit out by a calculator. He was simply supplying me with facts and offering some reasonable observations based upon those data.

"You should also know that I'm disappointed in you."

Okay, that last comment hurt. It was a piercing stab wound—no, a sharp, painful cut from a tomahawk. Suddenly, my high spirits began to descend.

"I was just bluffing," I told him as I sucked in the fresh Rocky Mountain air. "I never would have hit him with the hatchet, and I could certainly have outrun him if he decided to call my bluff."

"Nevertheless, I don't want you taking me for granted. I suspect that you really believed there was no risk, that if you had found that you miscalculated, you would have been able to rely upon me to step in and protect you from harm. You can't do that—that's courting disaster. People have lost their lives thinking they were immune from harm after learning of their guardian angels. They made the mistake of thinking that angels are omniscient and infallible. They aren't. There also are rules and standards of behavior that we abide by."

"I tell you very sincerely that I'm very, very sorry," I said. "I don't want you to be disappointed in me."

It was too nice of a day to argue, and I really was sorry.

Besides I wanted to talk about something that I considered more important—my efforts to establish some kind of telepathic link with somebody. Anybody. I had mostly been concentrating on Marco because he was an established telepath, or so Paul told me. I hadn't been making any progress that I could detect. I also occasionally tried to contact, telepathically, several of the well-known psychics who had established national reputations and who appeared regularly on television, even though I didn't hold them in very high regard.

In addition, I tried directing my thoughts to friends and acquaintances, but to no avail, since I never received any telepathic replies. Of course, I'm just assuming that the lack of obvious confirmation meant that those to whom I directed my thoughts never received them. I suppose it's possible that some messages might have gotten through but that I was never informed of such; I think it's extremely doubtful.

My usual pattern was to put aside an hour or so four or five days a week, use the relaxation techniques that Paul had taught me, settle into a comfortable position in a quiet corner of the house, and practice, practice, practice. If I ever became proficient at it, I thought, it was reasonable to assume that I would be able to carry on a telepathic conversation under everyday conditions and wouldn't have to cloister myself. But that would come later, I thought. There was also a good chance that such a day would never come because I just didn't seem to be making any progress. It was easy to get discouraged with no feedback.

"I suppose you know that I've been following your advice," I told Paul, "and have been practicing. I've really been trying to hone any latent psychic skills I may have. Quite frankly, I don't think I have any. I'm getting nowhere."

Paul was aware of my efforts and simply suggested that I keep trying. I asked him if there was anything he could do to help speed up the process, perhaps even spend time tutoring me, actually showing me what I should be doing, what I should be saying, how I could direct my thoughts toward a particular individual or how to go about actually receiving someone else's thoughts. The initial excitement of the prospect of developing such ability had worn off and the effort to develop it had become a drudge. If I could get some confirmation that the process was working, I could approach the project with renewed enthusiasm and vigor, I told him.

"Stop trying to read minds," he said.

I didn't understand.

"You're not fully opening yourself to allow the thoughts to flow freely, especially thoughts coming inward. Instead of trying to make yourself receptive to what messages others may be sending you, you're trying to read minds. You aren't a mind reader and you never will be."

Well, I could agree with that, but I don't think I ever entertained the notion that I was.

"Your approach is a bit anal, you know," Paul added. "Don't try to push it. Just relax, open up, and be receptive. The same thing applies, although to a lesser degree, when you are trying to contact others. Transmitting, if I may describe it like that, does require a bit more of an active approach than receiving."

Transmitting and receiving. I wondered if that made me some kind of two-way radio—a walkie-talkie.

"As for holding your hand and taking you step by step through the process—tutoring you—that is not the way things work. Practice is the best instructor," he said. "Have you ever heard that maxim?" Before I could respond, he continued, "You have to find the will and the resolve within if you want to reap the rewards. That is the only way you will become accomplished. It is a gift that, paradoxically, no one else can give to you. You must give it to yourself or you will never receive it."

"Maybe I'm not cut out for it," I said. "As far as I can tell, I have made no progress at all, and I have been working at it."

We had circled the pond, or lake—whatever it was. I had caught my breath and was about to start jogging again but instead stopped walking when a middle-aged woman who had approached us from the opposite direction spoke to me. She was about ten feet away when she called my name. She was dressed in a white halter top, white shorts, white socks trimmed in pink, and white athletic shoes. I don't know anything about such things, but I would guess that her hair was cut in a sort-of pageboy style. That is, it was rather short, coming down to about the neck and curled under. It was light brown with liberal strands of gray throughout, but also had streaks of a silver-blonde that most likely were artificially added for style. The effect was not unattractive.

She was on the tall side for a woman, almost my height, and it was obvious that she took some pride in her appearance. She was slender and athletic looking with no middle-age roll of flab showing on her bare midriff. In other words, the type of mature woman who probably would be the envy of friends and acquaintances, especially those fighting the eternal battle of the bulge, and those who wished they had the same kind of metabolism to retain their girlish figures.

The woman had brown eyes, a rather angular nose, lips neither thin nor full. I didn't notice any obvious makeup, and tiny beads of sweat made her face glisten slightly. She was neither beautiful nor plain. I guessed her age as somewhere between late forties and mid-fifties, a pretty wide range, but I'm not very good at such guessing games. I stopped when she spoke to me, as did Paul. She introduced herself as Sheila and said she had traveled more than fifty miles for the sole purpose of attending my lecture at the nearby hotel where the Golden Wings conference was being held.

"Do you mind if I walk with you?" she asked.

"No, that's fine," I said. "Actually, I was just about to do another lap jogging, but I'll walk with you if you prefer."

She agreed to jog with me. As it turned out she and I had similar workout routines in that we would jog until we became winded, walk until we regained our breath, jog some more, and repeat the cycle for an hour or so. Paul accompanied us, although he certainly wasn't doing the same work the woman and I were doing. Paul never worked up a sweat when matching me during workouts, no matter how strenuously I exerted myself. In fact, he never seemed to exert himself. Nor did I *ever* see him sweat, come to think of it.

After we had jogged halfway around the course, Sheila hadn't given any indication that she had taken notice of Paul. That likely meant that he did not exist as far as she was concerned. Nevertheless, rather than risk embarrassing myself by either mentioning him or by speaking to him, I decided to try to work the subject into the conversation.

"Is this your first time at this park?" I asked. "You said you live quite far from here."

"Oh, no, I've been here before. I come up this way on occasion. It's a beautiful setting, isn't it?"

There it was, my opening.

"Gorgeous," I said. "We discovered it yesterday when we were out for a walk. So we jogged for an hour and then came back again this morning."

We finished the lap silently and then fell into a walk again. We both took a minute to slow down the huffing and puffing.

"Who?" Sheila finally asked.

"Who what?"

"You said you were with someone. Is your wife with you?"

"Ah. No, it's a friend," I said. "An old buddy. A very old buddy, you might say." I gave Paul a look but he didn't acknowledge it.

"Did he leave?" she asked, looking around.

He winked at me and then just vanished. He didn't even fade to an apparition. He just disappeared.

"Oh, he's around someplace," I said nonchalantly. "He may have gone back to the hotel." It was the truth; I couldn't swear that he hadn't gone back. It certainly was possible, although I doubted it.

We walked and jogged a couple more laps while engaging in small talk until we mutually agreed that we should be getting back.

As we headed for the hotel, which was within sight, and where she also had booked a room, Sheila asked me if I could do her "a big favor." She had a manuscript that she wanted me to read and proffer an opinion. I almost groaned aloud. She was one of those, I thought. How I hated being put on the spot like that. Most authors who have been published eventually will be approached at least once—and most likely numerous times—by aspiring writers who want a free assessment of their literary works. I don't like to hurt their feelings, but I learned the hard way that it is best to say no at the very beginning. Not maybe, not perhaps, not "if I can find some time." It must be a clear and unequivocal no.

I'm no expert and I'm not qualified to assess the creative work of others. That was not the business I was in when I had a newspaper career; the two fields are distinct and separate, although there are some similarities.

I told Sheila quite bluntly that there was no time in my schedule for such a chore. I hated to do it, but this is one time when there is no substitute for brutal honesty. She seemed like a nice person and I liked her. Besides, she was visually appealing—sexy, if you will—and I enjoyed her company. But I vowed after the first time I was maneuvered and pressured into reading someone's manuscript that I would never allow that to happen again.

In that incident, when I gave my honest opinion of the piece as requested by the author—a friend of an acquaintance—she slapped my face so hard that I thought for a moment she might have dislocated my jaw. And then she began bawling; a terrible, shrill wailing that was as painful to the ears and nerves as the sound of fingernails being drawn across a blackboard. I was caught completely off guard by her reaction. Fortunately, we were out on my patio at the time and not in some public place like a library.

Thank goodness for small favors. Luckily, hardly anyone is home in my neighborhood during weekdays because most people work, so I wasn't too concerned about the outburst drawing undue attention. I was more concerned about the woman's well-being. I prayed, figuratively speaking, that she wouldn't faint or bust a blood vessel.

I was speechless. I instinctively reached out and laid a hand upon her shoulder to try to console her—but mostly to shut her up. Mercy, that wailing was unnerving me. She immediately batted away my hand and, again to my utter disbelief, she caught me with another roundhouse that landed partially on my left ear. That really hurt and my ear immediately began to ring so loudly that I thought surely it would be audible to bystanders if there had been any.

Now I was annoyed. I then figured that she must be a mental case, so I didn't say or do anything except step back and cringe in discomfort. Still sobbing, she snatched the bound manuscript from the patio table and stormed out of my yard, weeping all the way to her car parked in my driveway. As she drove away, my ringing ear thanked me that at least it was no longer being subjected to the woman's shrieks. That was some relief, although it still hurt like the devil for close to an hour afterward.

Needless to say, she hasn't spoken to me since, and the acquaintance who introduced us also has become distant and cold. That was the first and last time I ever allowed myself to be talked into critiquing someone's manuscript. A person could go deaf.

Thankfully, Sheila was understanding and took the rejection gracefully. We arrived at the hotel and went to our respective rooms. I took a short nap before getting cleaned up and dressed in less casual attire. I was about to leave my room to wander around the conference when the phone rang. Sheila asked me if I wanted to join her for a bite to eat. It seemed like a harmless enough request so I met her at a restaurant.

"How hungry are you?" she asked before we entered.

"Not very," I said. "But I'll sit with you while you have something."

"It's still a little early. I'm not really hungry yet, either. How about if we go to the bar and have a drink first. I could go for a vodka tonic."

"Sure, if you don't mind if I just have a diet cola," I said.

"Oh, that's no fun," she said, extending her lower lip in a flirtatious, exaggerated pout. "Come on, loosen up. You'll have a drink with me won't you? Pretty please, pretty please, pretty please."

Well, she was playful, interesting, and cute.

"Okay, I'll have one drink," I told her.

"Oh, goodie," she said, clapping her hands together in a little-girl gesture of glee.

We settled at a table facing each other, and Paul stood behind her. No one noticed him, and I pretended not to. I ordered a vodka and tonic for each of us. Sheila told me about her divorce and her two grown children, then asked me about my family. She finished her drink and ordered another; I was still nursing mine. She asked me about my books, travels, media interviews. She finished her second drink at the same time that I finished my first.

"Let's have another," she said.

"You go ahead," I told her. "I think I'll pass. We can talk."

"This is wonderful. I really wanted to hear your lecture, but I didn't know that I'd be spending the evening with you when I made my plans to come here."

She ordered another round. Oh, well, it couldn't hurt, I figured. I saw one of Paul's eyebrows lift when the fresh drinks were delivered. Sometimes he can be a pain in the rear, I thought, and immediately felt guilty about thinking it. The drink had relaxed me and I was feeling mellow. Oh, why not, I thought, so I started in on the second one. Sheila started looking more attractive and our patter seemed to be getting wittier.

She finished her third drink and ordered a fourth, which lasted just long enough for me to finish my second. Now I was feeling little pain and was enjoying our meaningless banter immensely. In fact, I began thinking she was quite the conversationalist, and to fete that sudden recognition I ordered another round, my third drink and her fifth. She polished that one off in no time but, lady that she was, waited patiently as the level of my drink gradually shrank while we chatted. When I finally got to the bottom of the glass, she quickly looked around for our server.

It suddenly occurred to me I truly was too uptight and rigid in my day-to-day living, that I should resolve to let my hair down more often, to have more fun. With that in mind, I didn't object when she ordered another round, but I made a mental note that it would be my last. Sheila was on her sixth and I was on my fourth. I was tipsy. Our hands were resting on the table only inches apart when she very deliberately and naturally intertwined the fingers of her right hand with my left.

This wasn't good, I thought. She was looking more physically appealing by the minute—or by the drink, actually—and her idle chatter began skipping along the edge of profundity. It was brilliant, deeply intense, insightful. At this point the part of my brain that controls higher functions—such as sound judgment—had already crawled off into some corner to take a nap. That left me at the mercy of what was still awake—and we know what's usually going on in there. I certainly was conscious of a robust physical attraction that I was feeling. It was becoming obvious where this evening was going to end if I allowed it to happen.

I don't know why but I turned my attention to Paul. His face was pretty much emotionless, but he very imperceptibly shook his head and mouthed the word "no" several times. Maybe he actually said it but if he did I didn't hear it. Talk about being conflicted! I tried to gently withdraw my hand, but she kept a firm grip.

"I'm married, you know," I said. My speech was slurred.

"So was I. So what? It doesn't bother me. And you don't have to worry, I can keep a secret," she said seductively.

Sheila was slurring her words. I had to admire her in a dubious, almost perverse, sort of way, though, because she already had five drinks under her belt, was working on the sixth, and she was still more or less able to keep herself from sliding under the table. With her smaller body, she had less blood than I have, which means that her blood-alcohol level would have to have been considerably higher than mine even if I matched her drink for drink. I had now finished only three drinks and felt that I would be on my face under the table if I finished the one in front of me.

Was this a regular routine with her? If it was, I wondered how she could continue to keep her girlish figure. Maybe the running was designed specifically to burn off those alcoholic calories.

Paul apparently had given up on me—he was gone. I knew that I was treading on shaky ground but the vodka had set up shop in my brain and by now was pretty much calling the shots, in a manner of speaking. It had tucked my more rational thought processes into bed, kissed them nighty-night, and had thrown open the door to some late arrivals to the party who had come to liven things up. I know them by the names Basic Instincts, Urges, Desires—you can call them what you will.

And then it hit me so suddenly that it almost knocked me out of my seat. The words were so clear and distinct that my first thought was that someone had actually come up behind me and spoken directly into my ears.

"Be careful! Leave! Excuse yourself!"

I visibly winced and snapped my head around to see who had spoken. Sheila and I were still alone. I was overwhelmed by a sheer sense of terror and yet there was nothing toward which I could point as the source. I felt the blood drain from my head. The fear turned cold as my brow and hands became clammy. My heart began pounding, my vision narrowed as though I were falling backward into a tunnel. I imagined that this must be how our primitive ancestors felt when they came face to face with danger in which they had to decide either to fight or flee. It was as though some organ or organs in my body had abruptly dumped a barrel of chemicals into my bloodstream.

But there was nothing to fight so my instinct was to flee, to run out of the room in blind, mindless terror. But why? What was there to flee from? I would look like a fool. I couldn't fight and I couldn't flee, so I simply froze. I was absolutely convinced without a doubt that I was dying. There could be no other explanation. So this was what it was like to have a heart attack or a stroke—whatever it was that had stricken me—and my life was going to end on a barroom floor a thousand miles from home, I thought.

"Are you okay?" Sheila asked, a look of alarm spreading across her features.

I wasn't, and I was probably as pale as an overcast day. I tried to control my breathing, which had become labored and shallow. I wasn't on the verge of panic—I had already gone well over that line. A steel band had clamped itself around my chest, constricting my breathing, and I was certain that my lungs weren't getting enough oxygen to deliver to my pixilated brain. Just at the moment when I was totally convinced that I was about to slip into a dark abyss of emptiness, that nothing could stop me now from going over the edge, the terror began to wane. I had peaked.

Ice cubes skittered across the slick surface of the table and the remnants of Sheila's vodka and tonic pooled briefly before beginning to flow in ever-so-slow rivulets outward. She had knocked over her glass with an elbow while still clinging tightly to my hand.

She stared helplessly, a look of distress in her eyes as I struggled for control. We both sat quietly for several minutes while I consciously and silently talked myself down from the episode. Gradually, the feeling of dread passed and I finally regained control. I nodded to her. She took the hand she was holding into both of hers.

"My God, you looked like you were going to jump out of your skin," she said, patting my moist hand. I couldn't tell her, but I suspected that it was the disembodied voice that I had heard with such clarity that started my panic event.

After I had regained my composure and convinced myself that I was not at death's door, I searched my thoughts for an explanation. I considered the possibility that I was going mad. How else to explain hearing a voice that isn't there? No, that would leave Paul out of the equation. And then I heard it again.

"Leave! Excuse yourself! You will regret it deeply if you don't, and it will change your life drastically."

But this time I didn't panic because I understood, and a soothing relaxation began settling over me, which had nothing to do with the booze. I still can't say to this day whether I actually heard the words—certainly Sheila hadn't—or if they were thoughts so strong, so precise, so pronounced and forceful that my brain actually interpreted them as electrical signals traveling through my auditory system. But I knew where they had come from.

It was Marco! He didn't have to identify himself. I knew because—well, because I knew, just as I knew that I had just been the recipient of an enormous privilege. I had received and understood a strong, clear telepathic message!

"I'm sorry," I said to Sheila, "but I have to leave. Thank you for the company. I enjoyed our visit."

I extracted my hand from hers, placed a $5 tip on the table—the drinks had been paid for as we ordered them—and went back to my room. I prepared for bed but lay awake for about an hour trying to re-establish contact with Marco. He had kept me from walking—stumbling is more like it considering the vodka in my bloodstream—down a perilous road, and I wanted to thank him. As far as I know, I didn't have any success.

Observation By Paul

"A moment of bliss for a lifetime
of contrition doesn't seem
like a bargain to me."

contact

After returning home, I got into the habit of working fairly diligently and with some regularity on trying to develop any extrasensory skills I might possess. In September I thought I had made some slight progress when whole, unarticulated, silent thoughts seemed to cross my mind. They were rather prosaic, even banal, signifying nothing, but I knew again deep in my bones that they were tidbits from Marco. He was working with me, helping me, giving me encouragement. Practice, practice, practice had become my mantra. Meanwhile, I wasn't seeing Paul as often as I had been during our so-called therapy sessions.

September rolled into October and I was growing impatient with what I perceived as the incredibly slow pace of my progress, which I had expected to increase exponentially after my first tentative success at receiving Marco's communication. I was hoping that I would be able to achieve a very high level of proficiency—at least equivalent to the degree to which I received the message in the Denver barroom. It seemed that at the pace I was going it would take forever to get to that point.

The last time I had seen Paul, late in September, I had asked him if he could arrange a face-to-face meeting between Marco and me. I felt that if I could sit down and talk with him man-to-boy, as it were, he would be able to offer me some words of advice, some guidance on how to speed up the process. I felt intuitively that I was capable of a high degree of proficiency—that was indicated in Denver. But I also needed to know if any of my thought-messages were getting through to Marco. While I was receiving some messages from the boy, I wanted to know if I was also successfully conveying.

Paul can be so mysterious at times, which also has the potential to drive me to distraction under the right circumstances. Or maybe I'm just too naive, unsophisticated, not smart enough to understand what should be plainly obvious. He declined my request without explanation and refused to provide me with any details when I pressed him.

"Why don't you just ask him?" Paul said. "If you are receiving from him, certainly he would be able to tell you if he has gotten any thoughts from you as of yet."

I just stared at him dully. I smacked my forehead with the palm of a hand. *What is the matter with me?* I thought. The answer was so blatantly obvious that I was almost embarrassed for not seeing it. I don't pay much attention to what most people think about me, if anybody thinks about me at all, but I wanted Paul to have a bit more than lackluster regard for me. Or, at the very least, that he not think of me as a dunce, something I was feeling like at that moment.

"In fact," Paul continued, "do you really need such confirmation? After all, Marco is a telepathic savant. They don't get any better than him. Clearly he is receptive to your thoughts based upon the barroom incident. Wouldn't you agree?"

It appeared that he was right again. But the circumstances were different, so perhaps it didn't necessarily follow that I was successfully sending. Now that I thought about it, just how did Marco know what I was doing and thinking while I was in the bar? He wasn't there to witness it. I knew from experience that Paul withheld things from me when it was in my interests or when he had other reasons to do so. However, while not deceptive, he definitely can be evasive and circuitous when he has a mind to be.

"You once told me that I am not a mind reader and that I never will be," I said.

"Yes, that's right."

"That was in the context of a discussion on telepathy. I concluded then that telepaths are not mind readers."

"A fairly reasonable—if not totally infallible—conclusion, I would say."

"If Marco wasn't in the bar and if I wasn't transmitting thought messages to him, how was it that he was able to warn me to stop and get out of that mess? After all, he's not a mind reader, is he?"

Paul smiled.

"That finally occurred to you, did it? I wondered if you would ever figure it out. But you apparently have, and I must say that I'm impressed. I commend you," he said.

"You disappeared right before I got the message at the bar. Could that be related in any way?"

It could, and it was, according to Paul. He had wanted to teach me a lesson while at the same time extricating me from a situation that had the potential to alter the rest of my life in a way that I would not find advantageous. In fact, it was more than just potential, Paul said. I had been on a slippery slope to tribulation and had avoided that destination at the last moment. He felt it crucial to intervene.

He declined to discuss it in any detail except to admit that while I was so preoccupied with the seductive woman, he had contacted someone—an "entity" he called it—who had contacted someone (another entity?) who contacted Marco, who transmitted the message to me without fully knowing the situation. Apparently, a lot of trust was involved. In short, the episode had been orchestrated by Paul to shock me out of whatever spell I was under.

I suppose he had a good reason to reach out to the intermediaries rather than sending the message himself. It never occurred to me to ask him the point, but I suppose the fact that I was essentially ignoring him at that time could have had something to do with it.

I spent a good portion of October bearing down seriously on trying to develop any paranormal skills I might have. I made regular progress in small steps. There were no big breakthroughs. In the beginning, the messages I received—I concentrated exclusively on Marco—were more like hunches, intuition. By the end of the month, I was receiving fairly well-formed ideas, although they were not structured as language. That is, they didn't come in the shape of silent words inside my head. They were more abstract, more cryptic—thoughts without form.

Though it seemed to be going slowly, even so I was able to receive enough information to confirm that Marco indeed had begun to receive my projections to him. By the end of November, every once in a while a thought would take the form of one or two sentences of silent words in my head. As 2002 came to a close, I had become fairly proficient, I thought, in reaching Marco.

January brought no improvement over the level of achievement I had attained by the end of December even though I was working harder than ever. I thought that perhaps I had gotten into a rut by restricting myself to practicing with Marco exclusively. It was time to branch out, to try to reach other telepaths. Except for one minor incident—I don't know if it can be called a breakthrough—about the middle of January, 2003, there has been no further improvement.

Contact with someone other than Marco came about after I had mentioned to Paul—I met with him twice during that month—that I seemed to have hit a plateau that I couldn't rise above. He suggested tactfully that perhaps I was not applying myself as diligently as I could, that perhaps I was unwilling to make the extraordinary sacrifice that normally is required when someone is determined to break away from the pack. He encouraged me to continue practicing.

"It can't hurt," he said, "and you may discover some improvement along the way."

I was irritated by the lack of progress because I sincerely believed that I was applying myself to my full potential. But I had to give his suggestions serious consideration because in any disagreement between us the odds were that he was right and I was wrong. So I stuck with it. At the same time, I sought his advice and counsel on how I might go about trying to reach someone other than Marco. He merely repeated the general rules, which I was already familiar with, about how to relax to help prepare the mind, to open oneself up, and a few other platitudes. In other words, his best advice didn't give me any new insights and didn't help me much as far as I could tell.

I tried a number of experiments, including trying to repeat the incident at the mall involving the young Asian woman, though I still wasn't convinced that that was anything but one big coincidence. Nevertheless, as Paul said, I had nothing to lose so I sat myself down in the same food court. I tried to replicate the previous conditions as much as was possible, sitting at a table with a diet cola. (The soda was merely incidental; I'm sure the formula is a closely guarded company secret, but I doubt that it imparts psychic powers to the consumer.) I also had my nose poked into a book.

I had no idea what percentage of the population would be considered accomplished telepaths—those who have developed their latent abilities, are aware of it, and actively engage in telepathic communication. That is, was it closer to one in a hundred than one in a million? Would I be able to randomly contact one if that person was in the mall at the time? Also, how far away would be too far for me to establish contact: down the street or halfway around the world? This was all new territory to me and it was patently obvious that there was so much that I didn't know. I made a mental note to try to sit down and have a long talk with someone who could educate me on these matters.

I sat quietly with my eyes closed and let myself relax. When I thought I was in the right frame of mind, I "listened" for any random thoughts that might be floating around. After about ten minutes, and not getting any indication, I tried randomly "transmitting," projecting thoughts to any other telepath who might be able to pick up my signal. After another ten minutes I switched again to "receiver" mode, then back again. I did this alternately about every ten minutes.

About an hour into the experiment, just when I was ready to call it quits and head for home, I thought I detected something. It might have been just a random thought that I mistook for something else. But, no, it started getting stronger. It was definitely a communication!

I became quite energized and had to force myself to remain sitting quietly so as not to draw any untoward attention. This was nothing short of amazing. It was a woman, definitely. I don't know how, but I could sense it. She was saying *hello*. She had received my random transmission. Any moment I half-expected to hear "breaker, breaker." But I wasn't hearing words; these were random, unarticulated thoughts. They grew stronger by the moment. I was having a physical reaction to the excitement, similar to the intensity of feelings I had experienced in the bar with Sheila, but without the terror. In fact, there was something approaching bliss, and my heart thumped and my breath grew short. I warned myself to be careful not to hyperventilate.

Yes, I was definitely receiving! Now there was no doubt whatsoever. A few words began breaking away from the jumble of thoughts and distinguished themselves as soundless speech in my mind. She was telling me that she had received my thought projections with great clarity. I didn't know if that was because of my ability to transmit, her talent to receive, or a combination of the two. But she congratulated me on my aptitude, which meant that I had succeeded in sending a strong signal.

I could barely contain myself. I looked around the half-full food court to see if there was any obvious indication of who the sender might be. No one stood out. If my signal was as strong as she indicated, then it was possible that we could have a dialogue, although there was still an imprecise element to the communication I was receiving. I had to do a lot of interpreting because it was a mixture of unheard thoughts and unspoken words. Soon they began to coalesce into simple phrases and incomplete sentences. But I could make sense of it, that was the important thing.

Who was she?
Friend.
Was she in the food court?
No.

Was she in the building?
No.
How old is she?
Young adult.
Was she single, married, widowed, divorced, engaged?
Single.
What did she look like?
Average.

I had to meet her. I didn't care if she was ninety years old and as ugly as a warthog, she was fascinating. This whole affair was remarkable.

Can we meet?
Sorry.

Was that a denial? Maybe she was sorry about something else. I wasn't sure what the word meant in this context.

I must meet you.
Can't do.
Where do you live?
Far.
I don't mind. I'll travel.
Too far.
No, it's not. I'll fly if it's too far to drive.

I waited. No response. Thirty anxious seconds passed. "What's your name?" I implored.

No response. I started to panic. I tried to force myself to concentrate, but all that did was cause me to become more anxious, which in turn interfered with my concentration. I was losing her, could feel her slipping away.

And then she was gone. The link was broken. I sat for forty-five minutes trying to remain calm in an attempt to re-establish contact. It was hopeless, of course, because my attempt to achieve a placid state was in fact, paradoxically, an act of desperation. Despite numerous attempts to renew the connection, to this day I have not heard from her again. She remains an enigma who entered my life for a few brief, mesmerizing moments, a mystery woman who has attained a leading role during periods when I indulge in fantasies and daydreams.

That also was the end of my progress as of this writing. The plateau I had reached was finite, it seemed. I could go no further, and so I have resigned myself to the possibility that I will never become a full-fledged telepath. Even my contact with Marco has become sporadic and has stabilized at what I consider an elementary level. However, using the general population as a standard, I have to admit that I have achieved something priceless, even if it is crude compared to the skills of accomplished telepaths. I consider myself extremely fortunate to have had the opportunity to communicate with the mystery woman, however briefly, and that I am still able to communicate with Marco at times.

Of course, I will keep trying to improve my skills. I suspect that "the important work" that lies ahead for me, as described by Paul, may require me to become even more skillful in this arena, and so I continue to hang onto a sliver of hope that some day new heights will beckon me to resume my climb. If that happens, I will meet the challenge enthusiastically, happy to abandon the plateau on which I am currently stuck.

Observation By Paul

"A fool seeks vengeance.
The wise man seeks justice."

lonesome journey

Everybody eventually will fall into two major demographics: the mourners and the mourned. Those who survive into old age do so at the cost of seeing most of their friends, relatives, and acquaintances die off. Those who are spared the grief of witnessing those deaths do so at the cost of being the ones lowered into the ground as those who survive them shed the tears of sorrow. I have reached a point in my life where more friends, relatives, and acquaintances are dead than alive.

In October of 2002, one of the last of my closest friends died shortly after turning sixty-seven. He was a retired *Los Angeles Times* reporter and the man who, as managing editor of a community newspaper, had hired me as a cub reporter in 1963. In recent years, he and I had two or three phone visits a week, each lasting about an average of an hour. Even though he was nearly a year younger than I, he was a wise man from whom I learned much over the years. I looked upon him as my mentor when we first met and that relationship developed into a friendship that lasted nearly forty years.

The last lesson I ever learned from him was priceless: He taught me how to die. When he broke the news to me on the telephone less than two months earlier that he had just received a diagnosis of a terminal illness, I reacted as one would expect—with shock, sadness, and despair. Yet he was the one who offered the consoling words to comfort me rather than the other way around. He talked about his philosophy of life, which in essence was complete acceptance of the reality of the fact that one is born, lives, and dies. He was totally prepared for that final phase of his life.

My friend accepted his fate with equanimity. As far as I know, he did not go through the four phases that terminal patients typically experience upon hearing the bad news. He did not go into denial, he was not overcome with fear, and he did not go through a period of raging anger. He went directly to acceptance and peace of mind. I marveled at his strength that allowed him to face death with such serenity and composure.

I have seen people of faith, who professed to believe in God, an afterlife, and heaven, face the same news hysterically, grasping in terror at any straw—even allowing themselves to be manipulated and exploited by quacks and charlatans—in a desperate attempt to forestall the inevitable. And yet my friend faced the same inescapable fate without benefit of such faith to sustain him, provide him comfort, and assure him that he was on a road to salvation in which he would be granted everlasting life. He was an atheist, and atheists face the great unknown alone.

My wife and I went to visit him once after the diagnosis and he talked about how his impending death had enriched his remaining days, had given him new insights on a host of matters, and had even strengthened his marriage. I admired him for his courage and was deeply moved by the aplomb and sense of peace he displayed. I made a date to visit him again a few days later on a Sunday morning.

But he slipped silently away on the eve of my planned visit as he reposed on the couch, surrounded by his family, watching the World Series on television, if I recall correctly.

"There was a time when I didn't know any people who had died," I told Paul shortly after the memorial service. "Those were such innocent days. Now, it seems that most of the people I have been close to during my lifetime are dead."

"It's the price one pays for longevity," Paul replied. "The price becomes steeper the older one gets."

I nodded in understanding.

The mourning period passed, as such things inevitably do, and I got back into the routine of my life. I traveled to Minneapolis in November to speak at an annual New Age event known as the Edge Life Expo. Paul was my only traveling companion and we spent a lot of time over that weekend together. I flew into the city on a Saturday, spoke on Sunday, and returned home Monday.

I was relaxing on the bed of my hotel room Sunday evening watching nothing in particular on the TV, when I began to wonder just how much influence any guardian angel has upon the day-to-day life of the one whom it looks after. Paul was "sitting" on the edge of the bed, but there was no telltale depression on the mattress to indicate any weight upon it. We had been informally chewing the fat on subjects ranging from life, death, destiny, world conflict, terrorism, health concerns, and any of a dozen other topics. Something during that discussion probably triggered a train of thought about angelic influence on everyday life, but I can't pin it down to anything specific. I put the question to Paul.

"Well, it can't be quantified," he replied. "It varies from one individual to another. There's no set ratio or formula."

"Okay, then how about my case specifically," I said.

"I repeat, it can't be quantified. I will say, however, that you have been a handful relatively speaking. Most protectors are not kept hopping the way you have kept me jumping from one crisis to another throughout your life," he said.

He was grinning slightly, but I think he may have been only half-joking. Because every day is different, he told me, the amount of time spent interceding in my affairs for my own good had varied significantly over the years. There are quiet periods of weeks, months, perhaps years when little intervention is required, while at other times there are clusters of events large and small that require much more attention. The incidents can range from the serious, such as posing a threat to my life and requiring major intervention, to mere annoyances that call merely for smoothing out a few wrinkles to protect my serenity and prevent life-altering frustration or aggravation.

I still wasn't satisfied with the answer.

"I accept that you can't quantify it," I said, "but can't you just take a wild guess? I'm curious about how much influence you have on my everyday life. Like, would it be a lot, somewhat, not much, just a little?"

"I can't tell you, but I can show you," Paul said, shifting his "body" around on the bed to more squarely face me as I lay with my head resting on several pillows propped against the headboard. It was weird to witness his shifting of "weight" on the bed without any indication from the mattress that anything was there.

"How's that?" I asked.

"I can leave you on your own for a while and intervene only and if you are facing serious trouble. That is, I wouldn't get involved in the minor events in your life that normally would call for some attention from me. My absence would give you some indication of my typical level of involvement."

That was an interesting idea, I thought. We didn't arrive at any agreement at that time because I wanted to sleep on it; it could be a serious step if I decided to accept his suggestion.

A short time later, about a week after Thanksgiving, I was driving from my house over to the local mall to do my Christmas shopping when Paul suddenly appeared beside me in the passenger seat. By then I had gotten fairly used to that little routine. The first couple of times it happened I nearly jumped out of my skin, and I mildly complained that he was going to give me a heart attack or at the very least cause a fender-bender.

We picked up the thread of our conversation in Minneapolis.

"Could there be any serious consequences if we did agree for you to go on vacation?" I asked.

"Nothing serious, no," Paul replied. "I would continue to be vigilant to try to guard you against catastrophe. I just wouldn't bother with the little chores that I sometimes get involved in to help your life run smoothly. You would have to deal with those yourself."

That didn't seem like such a challenge. I consider myself rather self-sufficient and quite capable of tending to my own everyday affairs without anyone's assistance. I couldn't see what the big deal was in that regard. Something else that Paul said piqued my interest, however.

"You said you would be available to *try* to guard me against calamity," I said.

"That's all I can ever do—try," he said.

He gave me a strange look.

"I think I'd better clarify our relationship," he continued. "I thought you understood it, but I'm getting the impression that you are laboring under some misconceptions. I do not and cannot guarantee your safety. You can't take it for granted that I can protect you from all harm."

"I still stop at all red traffic lights," I said.

"Yes, I know. I'm not saying you don't. But all people die

even if they do have guardian angels. Bad things, terrible things, happen to people all the time. You will die someday just like everyone else. I cannot prevent that. I can try to help when I see that you are in danger. But that's all I can do. I have always succeeded, but one day either I will fail despite my best efforts or I will not intervene at all. That is the nature of life—and death."

"I don't suppose you could try a little harder?" I said, trying not to smile. "I mean, this dying business—you couldn't pull a few strings, make an exception?"

"No exceptions," he said straight-faced.

"Pity."

I pulled into the parking lot of the mall but we didn't enter the main building. We opted to stroll around the adjacent outdoor promenades and concourses lined with shops.

"I have no idea when that will be," he continued. "Your death, I mean. I have no voice in that matter. I do know that on occasion I can shove you out of harm's way if you are about to step into the path of a fast-moving bus. But if you happen to fall off a ten-story building or catch a bullet through the heart, there would be very little I could do in such situations. Do you understand what I am saying?"

I understood clearly. No exceptions, angels or not.

"I can live with that—so to speak. So, let's try it then. What's the procedure?"

"There's nothing to it, really. I'll just not get involved in the little things for a while. I'll still be available for any possible major events that might threaten you. How long do you want to shoot for, a couple of months?"

"Will that give me enough time to make a comparison?"

"Perhaps."

"What can I expect to happen during that time?

"You might notice more little annoyances. The days might not go as smoothly as you're used to. You might become irritable and agitated more frequently. That sort of thing."

If that was true, then guardian angels are more intimately involved in the lives of their charges than I had realized. I had assumed that they played only a minimal role in everyday life and stepped in only during periods of critical need, perhaps once every few years. A skeptical noise escaped my lips as I blew a gust of air through them. It was a hard concept for me to swallow, and I wasn't buying it just yet.

I asked if his prediction was specific to me or reflective in general of divine protectors and the individuals they oversee. There are instances of wide variation between individual angels with respect to the extent of their involvement with their wards, but his statement could be considered a generalization applicable to many others of his kind, he told me.

I didn't think two months was enough time for me to determine if there would be any significant difference in my daily life, so I suggested that we conduct the experiment through March of 2003, approximately four months.

"Agreed," Paul said.

I finished my Christmas shopping in less than two hours, which might be impressive to some but was quite unspectacular since I had only two names on my list. Paul hung out with me for about an hour and then disappeared.

Later in the parking lot when I was trying to juggle a couple of packages while trying to unlock the door to my pickup truck I dropped the keys. I swore a mild crudity under my breath. Then I cracked my head on the side-view mirror when I bent over to retrieve the keys, which caused me to drop the packages. I let out a yelp plus a louder and stronger curse word. I noticed in the mirror that I had cut my forehead and was bleeding slightly.

Over the next several months, it seemed to me that I was a bit clumsier than usual; that there was more miscommunication with people that led to verbal disagreements;

that people I came into contact with in the normal course of the day—employees of stores, medical offices, banks—were surlier, less helpful; that I was not suffering fools as calmly as usual; that my patience was more strained, thinner.

It could have been coincidence, but my attention to these rougher moments—which on the surface may appear to be merely routine matters—was heightened. Was I having a harder time than usual? Were the days stormier? Was I less relaxed than normal, more anxious? Were people more uncivil, or was I becoming less tolerant and thus making bigger issues out of relatively minor events? Was it my imagination or were there instances of more raised voices than usual, more disruptions and complications involving routine matters, more frenzied and boisterous moments and fewer ones of peace and quiet?

Something seemed to be amiss, but I couldn't lay the blame with any great degree of certainty on the absence of Paul's influence. And I couldn't really build a solid case for any claim that the stress level of my life had been elevated a notch or two. The individual minor disturbances most likely would be regarded by most people as just the normal vicissitudes of life playing themselves out, but taken as a whole, they appeared to me, at least, to add up to something more.

For example, while on my daily exercise routine shortly after Paul went on "vacation," I had to cut my jog short and limp back to the house. It appeared that I had somehow twisted my left knee. Rest didn't resolve the problem and I had to abandon my regimen. I consulted a doctor, was not satisfied with the treatment, and became embroiled in a pitched battle that resulted in angry letters of complaint that I sent flying off to my HMO and state regulators.

Then the bank where I had my checking account, mortgage, and line of credit was gobbled up by a global conglomerate. I called the new organization to get a few simple questions answered—like the whereabouts of $3,800 that had mysteriously disappeared from my checking account. Just my luck, my phone call was routed to the resident Axis Sally whose sole job apparently was to see how much insolence she could dish out before the customer blew his stack and hung up.

I should have known that it was a mistake to ask to speak to her supervisor.

Naturally, it was a composite of Lizzy Borden and Ma Barker who came on the line after Axis Sally put me on hold for fifteen minutes.

So off went another flurry of angry, indignant letters to government regulators and a bank officer, who probably had a good laugh over the matter. Again, there was no response.

Actually that turned out to be a stroke of dumb luck. I was so incensed by the treatment at the hands of the sadistic wenches that I refinanced my mortgage with another bank—and got a significantly lower interest rate. I got much satisfaction when I closed out my loan and canceled my other accounts with the banking conglomerate.

Despite that bright spot of serendipity, however, an epidemic of minor misfortunes began to plague me, consisting of hot tea spilled into the lap, dropped telephones, misplaced keys, broken eyeglasses, jammed garbage disposals and overflowing sinks, a rain-soaked truck interior from a window left open, a quantum leap in annoying phone calls from telemarketers, computer crashes, and various assaults on the body including scrapes, nicks, cuts, bruises, burns. I was sure I was setting some kind of a world record for the largest number of trivial mishaps to strike one person in the shortest period of time.

I fired off another batch of biting letters when a replacement part for my kitchen range began malfunctioning again only a few months after I had paid $200 to have the appliance repaired. The service manager of the store where I had purchased the stove less than two years earlier informed me rather cavalierly over the phone that "we don't manufacture them, we just sell them."

A growing belief began taking root in my consciousness that good-old American values such as pride of workmanship, common courtesy, a cooperative spirit of community, were in the process of crumbling . Yet I was determined to see the experiment through to the bitter end. Besides, mere coincidence could explain the cluster of minor confrontations, accidents, incidents, episodes, and disagreements that seemed to be plaguing me. I couldn't really convince myself of that, but I had to admit to the possibility. Deep in my guts, however, I was pretty certain that the absence of Paul's influence was being felt quite dramatically.

On Super Bowl Sunday of 2003, my wife called out to me while I was upstairs watching "The Simpsons" television show while she had the downstairs TV tuned to the game.

"Could you come down here, please," she called out.

Great. Right in the middle of my program. I get grumpy when that happens. I could understand if it were a real emergency, such as if the kitchen had caught fire. But usually it turns out that she wants me to catch a tiny garden spider and put it outdoors or some such thing.

"What do you want?" I called back.

I was enjoying the show and I determined that I wasn't going to move. Besides, I didn't smell smoke, so it couldn't have been that important.

"Just come down, please."

"Sorry, no can do. What do you want? I'm busy."

She appeared at the door of the bedroom.

"The cops are here."

That got my attention. I jumped up, peered out through the drawn drapes and saw a cruiser with flashing emergency lights in my driveway.

"You called the cops on me?" I asked.

"Very funny. Just come down and see what they want," she said.

It was a Los Angeles County sheriff's deputy and he said that a witness had jotted down the license plate number of my vehicle and left it with a note on the windshield of a car in the local post office parking lot. The note claimed that I had scratched the other vehicle with my car. It was untrue, and I told the deputy so. Nevertheless, he threatened to charge me with hit and run if I didn't agree to pay for the alleged damages. He also claimed that he had inspected my vehicle in the driveway and found paint smudges and damage consistent with the violation he was alleging. I thought that was a pretty neat trick since it was dark out.

This had gone far enough, I thought as I looked around vainly for some sign of Paul—it was indeed the last straw. I was the camel and my back was broken. No more, I thought. I desperately wanted to drop to my knees at that point and confess to Paul that he had made his point. I wanted to call off the experiment, willing to admit that my guardian angel is in fact important to me even in everyday matters not involving life and death.

I don't like people coming into my house with guns. It makes me nervous. The first order of business was to do whatever was required to get this goon out of my house and off my back. The most serious trouble I ever had with the law was getting two or three traffic tickets in more than fifty years of driving. So I told the deputy that I would pay to have the other vehicle repaired. He was satisfied with that and he called the owner of the other car on his cell phone to tell her of my acquiescence.

I had no intention of paying, of course. I figured that something didn't smell right. I suppose it's possible to scrape another vehicle with one's own and be unaware of it, but it just seemed a little too pat. I mean, what was the purpose of driving to my house with emergency lights flashing and then leaving them on in the driveway? What were the neighbors supposed to think? Unless he was investigating reports of gunshots and a corpse in the driveway, that was sheer heavy-handedness designed to intimidate, I thought. That belief was reinforced the next day when I inspected my pickup truck—in full daylight, not with a flashlight in the dark—and found no such damage as he had claimed.

My purpose of agreeing to pay was merely a ploy to get the cop out of my house. When the woman who owned the other vehicle called several days later to tell me that the damage would cost nearly $300 to repair, I relayed word to her that I would be turning the matter over to my insurance company rather than paying her personally.

She thought that was a horrid idea and threatened to file a police report and charge me with hit and run if I didn't pay up. That made me even more suspicious because I had assumed a police report had already been filed. Otherwise, why would the sheriff's office be investigating? It sounded to me like collusion—she was using the same language employed by the deputy. I wasn't buying it, so I fired off another batch of pungent letters to the sheriff, the deputy's supervisor at the local station, and some politicians.

After I voluntarily submitted my truck to the other car's insurance company for inspection and photographs, its agent said he could find no evidence of my involvement. My insurance company refused to pay, and I never heard another word from anyone about the incident. Well, just one, as well as the letter responses from the politicians.

The deputy's captain called me and said that there must be some mistake—the deputy never claimed in his report that he had found evidence on my truck to support the charge. And, no, the deputy hadn't tried to intimidate me with the flashing lights, the threat to charge me with hit and run, the suggestion that I not involve my insurance company, and the offer to drop the matter if I paid up.

Liars.

Throughout February and the first two weeks of March I felt like a wanderer lost in an equatorial swamp constantly batting at swarms of insects that sought to dine on my blood. I was feeling the beady eyes of all manner of predator following my every stumbling move looking for an opportunity to strike.

By the middle of March, with two weeks still to go with my experiment, I was walking around in a perpetual sour state, which alternated with bouts of fury, frustration, and aggravation. If I were a superstitious person I would have thought that I had been jinxed, that a hex had been cast upon me. It was as if everyone with whom I had dealings had decided in a moment of conspiratorial lunacy to not only abandon every sound principle of customer relations but to take it to even further extremes by adopting attitudes of contempt toward the customer or client or citizen.

Finally, I could take it no more.

"Paul, I quit," I said aloud one morning around the middle of March. I was alone in my den/office after my wife had gone to work. I was openly calling upon him to show himself—along with some mercy—something I had never done. I had no idea if he would respond but this constant aggravation was pushing me toward apoplexy.

He materialized before my eyes, wearing, of all things, a long white robe that fell in loose folds to below his knees and covered his arms to his wrists, and a simple pair of sandals or shower clogs on his bare feet. Not surprisingly, he also was wearing a sanguine smile that I could easily have interpreted as self-satisfied if I had a suspicious nature. I was delighted to see him.

"Well, did you learn anything?" he asked cheerily.

Until this episode, I had always considered myself quite self-reliant, capable of getting nicely through life—even without the necessity of a wife, if that was to be how things worked out. (I hadn't been sure since the age of fifteen that I ever would take a wife—or, more accurately, if a woman would ever take me as a husband. That was based upon a casual comment my mother made to me on a day when I suppose I was being particularly difficult. "I pity the poor woman who ever marries you, you rotten son of a bitch," she had spat out in a menopausal moment.)

A few months without Paul had made me realize that self-sufficiency is a relative term. It works well when we are in our comfort zones—the insular little boxes that we inhabit, be it the kitchen, the workshop, the office—where we are in total control. But once we venture from those secure enclaves into that big world outside, no one is totally self-reliant.

Almost with a hangdog expression, I admitted this to Paul and confessed that I hadn't realized just how vulnerable I would be in trying to get through the day without some backup.

"Don't be so hard on yourself. Actually, you coped pretty well, all things considered," he said.

I'm glad somebody thought so. I thought I had done miserably.

I wondered how my life would have been different if he had not gone on vacation. Was it just a random string of minor irritants that had been plaguing me for the last several months? Or was this the way life normally would play out if not for the interference run by our guardian angels? At what point and during what incidents would Paul have stepped in to smooth out some of the rough spots? Regardless, I am quite grateful that we humans are blessed to have these sentinels. The last few months were thorny and it was difficult for me to conceive of going through every day of my life operating at such a high stress level.

I couldn't imagine that Paul's intervention would be required in every instance; there must be some problems that people are required to handle on their own. So the experiment, although being terminated slightly short of the original goal, did yield some valuable information: Angels do have a meaningful influence in the everyday lives of their charges. They aren't there just during periods of crisis.

Anyway, there was no need for me to feel that I lacked gumption for failing to see the experiment through, Paul said. If I hadn't sent out my SOS to him when I did, he would have contacted me because he had discovered something that required me to be notified. That helped to salve my bruised ego somewhat but the fact remained that I did throw in the towel. However, this bit of information helped soften the blow.

Now I turned my attention to what news he might have for me. If he was on the verge of contacting me, that could mean only one thing—something serious was in the air. And that was enough to get me psyched, my senses impulsively on full alert. Although I had managed to stay busy in retirement, nevertheless there are periods of boredom, and I usually welcome events that occasionally come along to spice things up. The thought that he might be offering me a chance to have a bit of stimulation, maybe even some element of danger—well, not too much, maybe just a tad—tickled my spine and titillated the imagination. What was he waiting for?

I studied his face for some sign that might telegraph his thoughts—a look of worry, uneasiness. Something. Anything. All I saw was calm and composed pleasantness. Well, he would get to it when he was ready and no amount of fretting on my part was going to speed things up. So I let myself relax and I visibly sank a bit deeper into my chair in front of the computer screen. In his own good time he finally got around to it.

"Don't do anything stupid in traffic," he said.

That was it? What the hell kind of "urgent business" was that? I would bide my time to see where this might go.

"I try not to," I replied.

"Right. There's no doubt that you're a defensive driver. That's good. What I mean is that you should make a conscious effort every time you get behind the wheel to keep your mind on what you're doing, to stay alert."

"Okay."

"Yes, I know, you always do—almost. Everyone has attention lapses though. I just want you to be aware of that. You don't have to be any more cautious than you normally are, just eliminate the lapses when you are driving. If there are any, of course."

"Will do."

I was deliberately being brusque and condescending.

"I don't want you to give the police any excuse to pull you over. Going broke from paying undeserved tickets would be one thing, but you might end up in jail, and that would be cause for concern," he said.

"What's this all about, then?" I asked, my interest now beginning to stir.

I was definitely disappointed to learn that no grand adventure awaited me, at least not yet, and that I wouldn't be slipping off to some exotic destination on a secret mission. He simply wanted to let me know that the deputy who had come to my house at the end of January was pretty sore with me.

It appeared that my letters of accusation had the effect of putting some law-enforcement officers in an uncomfortable position. It was possible, Paul said, that I could be singled out, kept under scrutiny for traffic violations, no matter how minor, to be ticketed. I had to admit that my old junker of a truck did stand out in my neighborhood, so it wouldn't be hard to spot. But I wasn't particularly worried, especially since I no longer had a daily commute. Most of my driving consists of running to the grocery store or the post office. Most of the time, my truck just sits in the driveway, sometimes a week or more at a time without moving. Heck, I probably rack up more miles on my daily walk than I do in my truck.

"What did I do to get them on my case like this? I didn't go looking for a fight, I just put up a fuss when I thought that I had been unjustly accused."

"When you complained to their superiors rather than roll over and meekly defer to them, they took it as a personal challenge to their authority."

He told me to try to imagine the following scenario.

A young woman parks her shiny new car—a cheap, low-end import, but new nevertheless—in the parking lot of a commercial center near my house, where I occasionally park when I go to the post office. My vehicle is neither shiny nor new. It is a 1982 Toyota pickup with nearly a quarter million miles on it. It has dents, dings, scrapes, a badly oxidized and splotchy paint job, a broken bumper, pitted windshield, a bit of rust, and leaky weather stripping around the doors and windows.

The interior isn't in quite that good a shape.

Somehow, the shiny car had acquired a scratch along the driver's side. On a day that I visit the post office, the woman decides that she wants to have the scratch removed. Because of the deductible, her insurance would not have covered the expense. She looks around and her eyes fall upon my pitiable heap.

It stands out like a gravy stain on a silk tie. Surely it can't belong to anyone of consequence in this neighborhood. More than likely it is owned by one of the illegal immigrant workers who travel to the area daily to perform the menial jobs that keep the middle-class neighborhood fit and functioning. Probably a gardener. Most likely uninsured.

She jots down the license plate number, taps a friend or lover or relative in the Sheriff's Department, and a deputy is dispatched to my house. Well, obviously the house doesn't belong to a migrant worker. Still, anyone who drives such a piece of junk probably wouldn't be very savvy and should be easy to squeeze.

I wasn't that squeezable. I put the heat on them and they got sore.

If I began getting undeserved tickets, I wouldn't be the first person to be targeted by cops with a grudge. And on a more serious note, Paul reminded me, there have been cases where innocent people have been hauled off to jail, have been hurt while "resisting arrest," and have died in custody under suspicious circumstances.

It was good advice. I promised to be on my best behavior and to remain alert.

"One more thing, though," I said.

"Yes?"

"Don't be a stranger."

Observation By Paul

"All mortals are stardust, an insignificant mass of atoms that comes together and develops awareness of itself. How sad that most people—those masses of stardust that have achieved consciousness—don't appreciate the miracle of that."

the cargo cult

My adventures with Paul were magical, nothing short of miraculous, and I am so very grateful for having been given the privilege to meet him, to get to know him, to interact with him, to learn from him. I was sorry when the period of the dynamic relationship with him eventually returned to the more sedate stage that I presume is the normal status between most people and their guardian angels. At the same time, I realize how extraordinarily fortunate I am to have been granted the honor of contact.

But after I had finished writing this diary about my adventures and read it over several times, it struck me as extremely odd that I could not remember one single time when Paul had mentioned the word *God*. It was not only odd, it was absolutely extraordinary. I looked through all of my notes, racked my memory, did a computer search for the word *God*—several times.

I wasn't precisely right. He had spoken the word on exactly two occasions that I could pinpoint, which still struck me as extraordinary considering the source. In addition, when he did use the word, it was almost in a generic sense, much as someone like myself might use it in general speech rather than reverentially or in a spiritual sense.

In one instance, I quoted him in an observation at the end of chapter six, and in the second instance he used the word in chapter eight when talking about love. Aside from that, he had never broached the subject even obliquely, had never once alluded to a supreme deity, as far as I could recall. Once that realization got to bouncing around inside my head, along with the minimal mention of God, other questions and reservations began taking hold and sprouting.

For instance, he never claimed to be a spiritual entity. I realize that might sound naïve because a guardian angel is, by religious definition, a spirit. But I am exploring beyond the spiritual realm here. One could imagine a definition of "guardian angel" that is broader and encompasses more than a religious or spiritual characterization. After all, there is a group of crime fighters that use that very name, the Guardian Angels, and its members are quite mortal citizen volunteers.

I'm sure that Paul must have known that I would naturally have assumed that he is a spiritual entity. But the fact remains that he never made such a claim—which would have been confirmation for me—and that leaves a gaping hole for me to at least raise the question.

A previous incident, nearly a year after I had first met him on Easter Sunday of 1999, is what provisionally had led me to the conclusion that Paul was a divine entity. Someone whom I unequivocally admire and trust revealed Paul's special relationship with me. Although she didn't specifically state so, the information she provided seemed to imply that he was a representative of the God whom the majority of Americans worship. At least the implication seemed clear enough to me. Now that I have gone back to re-read the incident as I chronicled it in my second book, the phrasing surely could have led me to no other conclusion.

So what was I thinking during all that time that I was in close contact with Paul?

How could I accept with apparent composure the seemingly miraculous events of his sudden appearances and disappearances, his ability to materialize as an apparently normal mortal visible to anyone or exclusively to me when he so desired, to dematerialize as an apparition visible only to me? How could I explain his evident intimate knowledge of details of my life going back to my earliest memories?

Any normal person observing such events would have no option except to explain them as supernatural phenomena. So how could I accept these events, which were observable facts, and reconcile them with my own beliefs—or more accurately, disbeliefs? Wouldn't I have to recognize that the very existence of Paul trumped my own convictions, that therefore I had no logical choice but to admit that my concepts were flawed, to stop denying that there really is a supernatural reality?

What a bizarre term that is, *supernatural reality*. It has to be the mother of all oxymora.

But I digress.

To answer all of those questions in one fell swoop, let me just say that I was simply waiting. I remember some years ago seeing a TV program about a tribe of primitive people, perhaps in New Guinea, who had lived in long isolation from the modern world. One day civilization came marching in with the construction of a modern airport large enough to accommodate jetliners carrying passengers and cargo. Hundreds of the primitive people on a daily basis pressed their faces to the wire fence surrounding the facility and watched in total open-mouth astonishment as the giant silver birds appeared from the heavens.

These semi-naked people, still living in much the same fashion as their prehistoric ancestors had for thousands of years, were quite simply thunderstruck. There was only one plausible explanation. The silver birds were instruments of the gods, the people they disgorged were messengers of the gods—demigods themselves, possibly—and the cargo was the riches of heaven sent for the benefit of a chosen people. No other explanation was possible. I am told that the incident (actually a series of incidents in several locations) later became known to anthropologists as the *Cargo Cult*.

To cash in on this bonanza, the natives used sticks and other crude implements to scratch out of the barren earth their own version of a runway, complete with a makeshift "control tower" inelegantly fashioned from whatever branches the jungle might yield. It was their intention to lure the silver birds to alight at their own reception area and to claim their rightful share of the gifts from the gods. I know it's hard to believe, but nary a one of those heavenly silver birds ever touched down on the natives' landing strip.

My situation with Paul was not unlike that of these jungle inhabitants with their spellbound faces pressed raptly against the fence.

There was one minor difference: I could understand the arrival and the departure of the silver birds without superstitiously grasping for a supernatural explanation. The natives did not have that advantage because they had been born into a totally alien world from the one I inhabited. I was exposed to a world of science and technology; they had no modern technology or science.

While I, too, pressed my face in awe and wonder against my own metaphorical chain-link fence as the adventure with Paul unfolded before me, I was far better equipped. Thanks to an accident of birth that plopped me down in America, I had the ability to consider a number of options to explain the experience without jumping to the conclusion that it had to have a magical or supernatural base.

So back to the question of what I was thinking during my time with Paul. The answer is, nothing. I was reserving judgment. I was waiting—neither denying nor accepting the premise that he was a spiritual being—waiting to be convinced or persuaded one way or the other. To believe that he is a divine entity without any evidence or proof to support that conviction requires a leap of faith that my brain is incapable of making. When it comes to faith versus science, it is in my very nature to come down on the side of the latter. I require evidence. That's just who I am.

Well, what other explanation could there be? my primitive brain might ask.

I don't know. I have plenty of other questions, but I have no answers. But let us suppose for a few moments . . .

Let us imagine that countless other planets in the universe are inhabited by intelligent beings. Let us also assume that some portion of those inhabitants have created civilizations and that some portion of those civilizations are far ahead of the human species scientifically and technologically. Let us further assume that some of those advanced beings are space travelers capable of traveling to other worlds. Thousands of people have offered personal testimony over decades that they have witnessed or experienced a variety of contact experiences with extraterrestrial intelligence.

In addition, there is hard-core belief among various groups and individuals that this government, and perhaps others, are secretly in possession of rather large amounts of evidence that would support claims of extraterrestrial/human contacts. They also believe that other evidence exists in the public domain that scientists refuse to study for political reasons.

Although I am not of that opinion personally, I mention it as a counterbalance to my own beliefs. I personally know of no hard scientific evidence to support the testimony of those who claim extraterrestrial contact or even to assume as yet that such life does indeed exist. Yet despite what I consider to be a lack of scientific data, I am a firm believer in the existence of extraterrestrial intelligent life. Some may characterize that belief as faith, but my convictions are not faith-based; they are more substantial than that.

One does not require a leap of faith to imagine it: If such life does exist elsewhere, it would be in the natural order of things, quite in line with the laws of the cosmos as we thus far know them; a supernatural explanation would not be necessary.

Now let us presuppose that the inhabitants of some of those civilized and technologically advanced planets have evolved into creatures with a highly developed moral, ethical, altruistic sense—beings whose very nature is gentle, kindly, compassionate and, most of all, benevolent. It is not illogical—perhaps a bit farfetched, but not impossible—to imagine that one of those space-faring species could have stumbled upon our tiny little corner of the universe in its travels.

Some religious orders on Earth send out missionaries to tend to the needs of the less fortunate scattered in countries around the globe, as well as to seek converts to their own religious beliefs. The governments of many developed nations also have programs designed to give aid and comfort to needy nations. Private secular groups as well are actively working to alleviate human suffering and improve lives of wretchedness.

If I really let my imagination loose, I can visualize a race of extraterrestrial space travelers whose technologically advanced civilizations provide for every need of its citizens to live long lives of comfort and contentment. But perhaps somehow that is not enough to satisfy deeper yearnings. I'm not knocking luxury, something that probably most humans would cherish. But suppose there is still an inner emptiness that mere physical comfort and wealth cannot fill, a driving need to find some greater purpose in their lives. Imagine that these millions, or billions, of individuals discovered that they could fill that internal emptiness through genuine service to others—that their lives would have greater meaning if, instead of going monotonously through endless hedonistic days of self-indulgence, they dedicated themselves to trying to help others who are in need.

So this is one of the many places where my imagination could lead me: A race of "guardian angels" whose individual members devote themselves to the benefit of other sentient beings. No other reward other than a sense of satisfaction is sought.

I can imagine Paul being one of those selfless individuals. Of course, I would have to assume that the members of that species have mastered the art and science of communication by telepathy, the ability to become visible and invisible at will, a facility to probe the thoughts—perhaps even the memories—of those over whom they stand watch.

But, of course, that's all speculation. I just wanted to present at least one plausible natural alternative to explain Paul's presence as a counterpoint to those who might consider me astoundingly naïve, even stunningly simple-minded not to have immediately embraced the "undeniable truth" of Paul's supernatural pedigree. And I'm sure there are many other possible explanations that wouldn't have to wander into the arena of the supernatural. But since Paul did not provide me with a *curriculum vitae*, I can only speculate on his origins and background.

But even with the presence of protectors, there still exists much wretchedness and injustice in the world. So why are some people more fortunate than others? Why was I chosen to meet my benefactor while billions of others never get that opportunity?

Because life is not fair.

Other than that, I just do not know.

While writing these words, a long-distant memory suddenly and inexplicably popped into my head. I hadn't forgotten about the incident, but it had been lying dormant. This was the first time that it had come into view in several decades. For a period of a few months in the Army, while I was waiting an assignment to a kitchen after completing cook school, I served temporarily as a driver. I was dispatched one day to the site of a field exercise to pick up three soldiers and transport them in the jeep to headquarters. It was a routine assignment as far as I was concerned.

I had no idea what the three were frantically discussing in Spanish as I made the delivery. Only later did I learn that the body of another soldier had been found some hours earlier, beaten and stabbed to death. Apparently he had been bushwhacked as he walked from the Soldiers' Club back to his barracks the night before. While the troops were in the field on their training exercises that bright morning, an inspection of every troop's locker was conducted base-wide.

This search yielded bloody clothing from the lockers of the three recruits who were in my jeep. They were murder suspects, and yet no hint of that status was given to me when I received the assignment. When I found out about it later, I was really annoyed. After all, I didn't go to Military Police school, for heaven's sake, I went to cook school. As far as I was concerned, these three guys could easily have slit my throat, taken the jeep and hightailed it in a panicky, desperate bid to escape their fate.

Yet Paul had never mentioned that event during our discussions about the times he had come to me during perilous moments. Again, this gives me pause. Suppose he isn't a spiritual entity who has been with me for a lifetime? Maybe he is a mere mortal—albeit a very advanced one—who has the ability to tap into my thoughts. But if the memory of that very serious and potentially hazardous situation wasn't in my thoughts—and only now has resurfaced—then he wouldn't have been aware of it.

Thus he wouldn't have mentioned it. And he never did.

There are still many questions. In the meantime, I wait.

Observation By Paul

"Too many people spend too much time trying to settle old scores when they should be concentrating on the game coming up."

occasional visitor

I haven't had any further trouble with the cops. But when I'm out running errands in my pickup, it's nice to know that Paul is in the passenger seat, or at least I presume he is. I don't see him often any more.

Marco and I make contact every now and then. I continue to practice, to try to develop my telepathic skills, but not with the same intensity or fervor as before. I have made some further rudimentary contacts with other telepaths, but nothing so dramatic as to convince me that I am making breakthrough progress. Frankly, I am fairly certain that I am never going to advance much beyond the point where I currently am.

However, I'm not terribly disappointed. It's still fun and exciting whenever I do pick up a signal or get acknowledgment that someone else has received a communication from me. Hearing from a totally new person is particularly stimulating. That usually happens on a random basis, but I have reason to believe that there is a whole network of journeyman telepaths around the world who are constantly in contact with one another. Their numbers run into the thousands, I have heard. At least that is what is rumored among those of us who have rudimentary abilities but who are not proficient enough to become part of the network. It is said that an expert can join the dialogue on the network as easily as logging onto an internet chat room and joining the conversation.

I often find myself daydreaming about how marvelous it would be to have the skills to join such a group. But even if I never advance to that level, I am grateful for the rudimentary skills that I have been given and for the experiences that they have afforded me.

Mel has sent word that Eddie Dwyer's mutt was run over and killed by a car. The big man apparently was relating the news to Mel in a bar when he lost his composure and started blubbering like a little girl.

"He just buried his head in his arms on the bar and sobbed his heart out," Mel said.

"He changed after the fight. He grew real quiet. He doesn't seem to have a chip on his shoulder any more, and we've had some real nice conversations at the bar. He's really not such a bad guy. He invited me and my wife over to his place for a barbecue. We're going to go.

"Anyway, when he started crying for his dog, I just felt so bad for him. He's such a big guy. I never saw a big guy cry before. I thought I was going to start bawling myself. My throat got all tight and I really choked up. I put my arm on his shoulder in sympathy, and the next thing I know I'm holding him in a hug while he's crying."

I reached for the Kleenex as I read Mel's note. I should have listened to Paul but I had been too pig-headed. What had I proved, that I was now a better man than Eddie? That was obviously not true. A heavy blanket of remorse settled upon me as I came to realize that I had simply traded places with him—I had become the bully whom I once despised. I felt like a wretch, and at that moment I finally understood why Paul had been so opposed to my course of action. I dabbed at my eyes with the Kleenex and with a mixture of guilt and contrition vowed silently to put more trust in Paul's advice.

However, Paul has made himself pretty scarce lately. It's not as though anything has come between us or that we aren't on speaking terms. He just believes that I have gotten through the crisis that he insists I was facing and that it is time for him to melt into the background and out of sight. I still disagree with his contention that I was in dire need of his intervention in the form of talk therapy, but I certainly have no regrets whatsoever that he acted upon that belief.

He still hasn't divulged what "important work" awaits me, and I don't bother asking or even thinking much about it anymore. Whatever it is, I'm sure I'll understand at the appropriate time. For that matter, I don't even know when or if I will ever see him again, although every once in a while he makes his presence known to me—audibly, visibly, or sometimes just as a subtle but very real feeling detected by a sixth sense. I suspect he'll stay in touch. If not, just the knowledge of his existence has made a profound change in my life, and I know he will continue to be there until I take my last breath.

After that, I'm not certain of anything.

Observation By Paul

"A guardian angel is not a nursemaid. I help at times but you are ultimately responsible for your own destiny."

Epilogue

I began compiling notes—actually, keeping a diary is more accurate—shortly after Paul showed up in my gazebo in November of 2001 and I continued doing so until the adventure just fizzled out in early 2003. In April of that year, I began to periodically work on the notes to try to organize them into some kind of coherent story. As the months rolled by, a manuscript of sorts began to take shape. After a year or two, I considered the project finished and I put it aside. For some reason that eludes me, I didn't make any attempt to market the manuscript and it reposed dormant in my computer until sometime early in 2006, if memory serves.

Perhaps I considered it to be just what it began as—a private diary for my eyes only—or that the information was somehow privileged, too personal to share. Then again, maybe I thought the manuscript wasn't marketable, that there wouldn't be much interest in it. Whatever the reason, the fact remains that I simply set it aside.

But then an occasion arose where I happened to show it to the CEO of Origin Press, which had published my second book in 2001. He expressed an interest in it, but I was still reluctant. Over a period of months, perhaps a year, in a number of phone conversations and e-mails, he invariably inquired whether I had changed my mind. I hadn't. However, in April of 2006 I did have a change of heart and agreed to submit it for publication.

For reasons peculiar to the publishing business—which I know nothing about—the project got off to a fitful start and it was on-again/off-again for more than a year. During those fits and starts, I worked on polishing the manuscript during the on-again times, put it aside during the off-again times, and repeated the process several times. Finally, sometime in the fall of 2007 I got the final go-ahead, with a January deadline and a planned publication date for June of 2008.

For several months I rewrote and polished, shipping the pages off to the publisher as they became available for editing, which he then sent back to me with corrections, suggestions, and revisions to be incorporated into the manuscript. At last, the day arrived when I deemed the manuscript to be complete, ready for one final look by the publisher before going off to the printer. I finally hit the send key on Monday, February 11, several weeks behind schedule, launching the final draft into cyberspace, destination Origin Press.

Paul and I hadn't visited much for years, and it had been well over a year—probably more—since our last contact. When we had been meeting on a regular basis, I had become accustomed to his abrupt comings and goings. However, the recent hiatus apparently had lulled me into a less anticipatory state, to a certain degree, in which I wasn't very primed for his sudden appearances. That's probably the reason that I recoiled when a soft voice, spoken directly into my ear, sent my spine a-quivering.

"So you're actually going ahead with this, are you?" he asked. He was standing directly behind me, bent over my shoulder peering at the computer screen.

"Jeepers, I really wish you would give me some advance notice before you do that," I said after my heart had settled back to a rate comparable to that of a nervous rabbit.

It was not surprising to me, of course, that Paul would know about the manuscript and my plans for it. Most likely he had been there reading over my shoulder all the time that I was putting it together. As such, I wasn't sure if his question was mere rhetoric or if he really was seeking information. I leaned toward the rhetorical explanation on the assumption that there wasn't much about me that he didn't know.

I swiveled around in my chair in front of the table that holds my computer equipment and planted my feet on one of two medical-office stools that I keep in the room. Paul settled down on the other one by my desk. I leaned back and cupped my hands behind my head, hoping to assume a casual demeanor to disguise the defensiveness that I was feeling. I had made commitments regarding the manuscript, after several years of hesitancy, and I had the feeling that Paul was going to argue against the project. Otherwise, why would he be showing up now right when I was on the cusp of finalizing it, particularly since I hadn't seen much of him in several years?

"Yeah, I think it's an interesting story," I said, "and I finally decided, after much contemplation, that I'd like to share it."

I was going to ask him if he had any objections, but then thought better of it. So I fiddled with a ball-point pen instead, hoping that my laid-back masquerade was working. I wasn't sure how I'd react if he did express misgivings, but I didn't want to give him an opening. If he had something to say that I didn't want to hear, let him do it without my help.

"You've thought it through as best you can, I presume," he said. "But I don't know if you've considered all of the implications."

"I think I have. Why, what do you have in mind?"

Damn. So much for my resolve not to give him an opening. I had just done it.

"First, there's the dialogue. Don't you think readers are going to doubt that you have the ability to remember with such accuracy the actual words that were spoken by me and others over a period of several years? You didn't take notes and you didn't record the conversations. When you put quotation marks around words, it indicates that those are the exact words that were spoken. I would say there's a high degree of inaccuracy there."

"I presume you've read the manuscript," I said.

"I have."

"Can you point out one instance where the quoted material does not accurately and honestly capture the thoughts, the tenor, and the nuances of the speakers' words without any bias or distortion?"

"That's not the point."

"What you probably don't know, because I haven't written it yet, is that the book will contain an explanation of that very thing. The quoted material is an approximation of what was said, and the reader will understand that."

"That's good, being open about it. Now, another thing I'm curious about: What was the deciding factor for your ultimate decision? I know you weren't too keen on the idea for a long time. Why the change of heart?"

It was a tough question, and I'm not sure I could provide a satisfactory answer. Certainly it wasn't the money. I don't accept royalties from my publisher. I encourage him to sink any such funds back into the business so that he can continue to bring out important books. It certainly wasn't for any small bit of fleeting fame that might come my way. I value my privacy and I don't particularly care for the attention that the books draw to me.

The brooding look now wrinkling my brow didn't do much to reinforce the breezy attitude I was trying to maintain; surely it couldn't have escaped Paul's notice. I suppose if I had some time—maybe a week—to think about it, I could have come up with a fairly reasonable answer to his question. But at the moment, it totally eluded me. I could only guess.

"Dunno. Maybe I just couldn't resist the charisma and persuasiveness of my publisher," I said with a sheepish smile.

"Uh huh," Paul said with almost a snort. "Well, be that as it may, let me ask you this: What good is it going to do you?"

I pulled my feet off the stool and turned to stare Paul directly in the eyes.

"Before I answer that, why the third-degree, why are you so interested in my motives? Do you have any reservations about the project? Are you trying to talk me out of going ahead with it?" I asked resolutely.

I already had given him the opening that I vowed to myself that I wouldn't so I didn't see any point in trying to continue the charade at this point. Frankly, I was becoming a little annoyed, perhaps because I felt that he was prodding me, putting me on the defensive. I was of a mind that I didn't need to justify my decision to anyone, including Paul.

"Believe it or not, I'm only thinking of your best interests," he responded quietly. "No, I have no objections to the book if that's what you really want. I'm just concerned that you may be placing yourself in a position that could subject you to a lot of stress. I simply don't want you to fall into that same situation I found you in back then . . . you know."

He gave me a quizzical look and a nod, as if to ask if I understood. I did. I could see that we were back at that old disagreement again, the one where he feared that I might be suicidal despite my steadfast insistence that he was far off the mark. I will admit that I had been feeling pretty crummy back then—what was it, over six years ago—compared to how terrific I was feeling these days. Maybe the talk therapy, my meetings with Paul over a period of about eighteen months, had something to do with the transformation. Or maybe it was just the good old passage of time—which I understand heals all.

"Have no fear," I said, "I'm fine and I intend to remain so."

"What do you think reader reaction will be to your book?"

"Mixed, as usual. But I have a feeling that you're talking about the ones who will think I'm loco, and whether that's going to put me in a funk again and require another intervention by you."

"Very perceptive . . . and also inadvertently revealing. You practically admitted that my intervention was required. You didn't say *elicit* or *trigger* an intervention, you said *require*. That undercuts your previous protests and denials about the need for me to step in when I did."

He was right, of course. Call it a Freudian slip, or whatever, but I now believe that my psyche had spoken. Had I really been feeling so rotten that I did need—no, require—Paul's help to deal with my emotional turmoil? Had I been kidding myself all along? I took a moment to truly examine my innermost thoughts and feelings, the ones around which I had posted an almost impenetrable defense of bravado and machismo. I lowered the guard and took an honest look, and was mildly shaken by the view. He had been on the mark all along. I actually *had* needed him at the time he made his initial appearance in the gazebo, and I was now willing to admit it—to myself.

Nevertheless, that was then, and this was now. The circumstances were quite different; he was comparing apples and oranges. Previously, I had been reeling from the 9/11 attacks, which had dealt a severe emotional blow to the whole nation while causing the termination of a crucial project of mine, and I certainly wasn't immune from being traumatized. What we were dealing with now, however—or at least what Paul seemed to be focused upon—was how the reaction to the book from a certain element of critics would affect my outlook.

"Hey, just Google me and you'll discover that a lot of people are saying a lot of things about me, as you probably already know."

I thought he was enormously overestimating my fragility. I'm not a porcelain doll. If I were twenty-five and looking to impress the girls, trying to find a good job, building a career, I probably would have had some interest in what others thought or said about me. But I already have a girl, am retired from a nifty job and career, and I'm seventy-three years old. Many things that seem so earthshakingly important when we are young tend to fade into insignificance when we reach the autumn of our years.

"Say, is this another talk-therapy session?" I asked after the notion suddenly popped into my mind.

Paul flashed a smile and a look of amusement.

"Not really. I can become just as curious as the next . . . person. Don't be so defensive," he said cheerily, "this is just a friendly visit. However, if you have anything to get off your chest, I'm willing to discuss it with you."

"As I said, I'm fine. Unless you think I'm wacko for sitting here talking with some imaginary entity."

I had to grin at that one. Paul let loose with a hearty laugh, perhaps sharing the ludicrous, and hilarious, scene that the statement conjured up, at least in my mind's eye. I mean, here's the joke: A guy is talking to an imaginary friend, and the friend says, "You're nuts, you know." And the guy asks his friend why he would say that. The friend replies, "Because you're talking to me, and even *I'm* sane enough to know that I don't exist."

It tickled my funny-bone.

Maybe you had to be there.

"Yeah, you'll probably be okay," Paul said. "You're obviously in good spirits at the moment, and I think the vicissitudes of life aren't going to be as threatening as they once were. I suppose you can give some credit to the seasoning that comes with age.

"Well, you have things to do, so I'll let you be."

With that, he stood and it seemed evident that he was on the verge of taking his leave. I was disappointed. I was reminded of how much I had always enjoyed our time together, and I didn't want him to leave just yet. I grappled for some words to delay his departure.

"You know, I'm not sure I believe that everyone has a guardian angel!"

The words were out of my mouth while my brain was still trying to think of something to say. I didn't even know at the moment if I believed that, or even where the comment came from. All I know is that it got Paul's immediate attention. He sat down again, an inquiring look on his face.

"If you meant to be provocative, you've certainly succeeded," he said. "Okay, something's on your mind, so let's talk about it."

Crikey, now I felt like a condemned man who had just been strapped into the electric chair and asked if I had any last words. I mean, such an occasion seemed to call for something more than just idle chatter from the condemned about what a cozy place the warden had there. If I knew why I had blurted out my doubts about guardian angels, conceivably I could follow up with a *bon mot* of some sort, or at least something credible to justify the remark. I squirmed and stammered momentarily, and suddenly the germ that had triggered the statement came rising out of the depths of my memory like an express elevator.

I put my feet back up on the stool and assumed a more relaxed, but assertive, attitude.

"Let me ask you this. You had implied that somehow my application for a job at the *Times* happened to be sitting on the top of the pile just at the very moment that the copy desk supervisor needed to hire another editor."

"That's not the question, right?" he asked drolly.

The comment brought a smile from me and a reminder of the teasing, the interplay of words and wit that invariably became a component of our conversations, even despite the seriousness of them at times. My impulsive comment as he was preparing to leave—despite any deeper meaning—certainly did have the effect of keeping him around. That pleased me.

"Seriously," I said, "wasn't someone deprived of a job because it went to me, possibly because of your intervention? Maybe you and the other person's angel clashed, and you won, which was a win for me and a loss for the other guy. Or is it just simply that not everybody has a guardian? Maybe just some us lucky ones do?"

Paul leaned backward on the stool, his elbows and forearms tucked back onto the desk as he faced me.

epilogue   211

"Hmmm, I see your point. Yes, it would be unseemly for two angels to get into a turf battle. So you think someone got a raw deal because you have a guardian and the other person doesn't, is that it?"

"Well, it does beg the question of what happens when two or more angels have incompatible interests. How do they reconcile their differences?"

"You're assuming there were winners and losers. Who were they?"

"I won and everybody else lost," I said.

"Really? Your supervisor also won; he got the editor he was seeking. The job had opened suddenly and he needed to fill it quickly; you lived nearby and were available immediately. Those were two key requirements, which automatically eliminated the bulk of applicants. Incidentally, that would have included you if you were from out of town.

"Your desk mates won because you were able to carry your share of the workload; more of that burden would have shifted to them if a less qualified person had been hired. Maybe they and the supervisor thanked their angels for that little blessing. I'm sure the supervisor also got credit for saving the newspaper time and money because the *Times* didn't have to pay for transportation, lodging and meals for a string of two-week tryouts from out of town."

"I'm not saying that I wish someone else had gotten the job," I said. "It's just that it seems to me that guardian angels would have to lock horns in certain situations. If that is inconceivable, then an alternative would be that some people don't have angels looking after them."

"Wrong on both counts. We don't do battle—lock horns, as you put it. Sometimes we confer. No one got the job for you; you got it yourself. Besides life is full of disappointments, guardian angels or not."

I was starting to regret even beginning this conversation. It wasn't going anywhere that I had any real interest in visiting. The brutal—and selfish—fact of life is, I didn't care if I had started with an unfair advantage going into the competition. I was just glad that I had gotten the job instead of someone else. It had altered the course of my life, and I was happy with the outcome. I now wanted to wrap up the conversation, but Paul still had a few more things to say.

"And there weren't any losers," Paul said. "Those who weren't offered a tryout lost nothing. They simply went on with their lives, oblivious to the processes that went on at the *Times*. Do you see my point?"

Call me obtuse, but, no, I didn't. However, I respect Paul, so I give him the benefit of the doubt and assume that his line of reasoning is impeccable and that his conclusion is a valid one.

The conversation essentially ended on that note. I wish I could say that he left me with a lot to think about, but only two things came to mind.

Angels don't do battle, they confer. To me that means: Diplomacy over war under all circumstances.

And the second thing?

I've been very lucky.

Postcript:
An Update on the Contact Project

Although this chronicle is meant to stand alone and distinct from the author's two previous books, *The Contact Has Begun* and *The Challenge of Contact*, there is nevertheless a tangential link between them. With that in mind, this seems the right place and the appropriate time to present a brief update for the benefit of previous readers on what has been called the *Contact Project*. Many of them have raised questions and expressed keen interest in finding out what if any events or communications may have transpired in the long interim since the author's last book in 2001.

You'll recall that hundreds of humans from all races and nationalities of humankind were secretly contacted by the Verdants, a very advanced ET race, as part of the Contact Project; these contactees were known either as ambassadors or deputy envoys. As far as can be determined, 100 percent of the ambassadors and deputy envoys have remained publicly unidentified, although about a dozen or so people have approached the author claiming ambassadorial status. Most of them could not support their claims during routine questioning and/or vetting of their credentials. However, at least two have established themselves as completely authentic.

One of them personally delivered a momentous message to the author in March of 2001 at a major UFO conference in Laughlin, Nevada. This message indicated that, after lengthy discussions between the ambassadors and the Verdants, a date for the contact had finally been set and that he, the author, would have the honor of announcing it. The publicly available record shows that on August 25, 2001, the publisher pre-announced the author's keynote speech at the UFO Expo—which was to occur on September 16, 2001—during which the author was to announce the good news. As is well-known to those who have followed the author's story, on the evening of 9/11 the ETs abruptly suspended the formal contact between themselves and the human species. Crisis conditions on Earth required that the Contact Project be put on indefinite hold. Readers of *The Challenge of Contact* will recall that the author reported on this entire drama in that volume.

Since those days, there have been no more face-to-face or telepathic contacts between the author and the Verdants. But one major development is pending that readers of the Contact books have a right to know about.

A second claimant who passed muster first contacted the author in April of 2006. He was an intriguing fellow who held prominent social and business positions and whose credibility turned out to be impeccable. The author, who approached all such correspondents cautiously and skeptically, began a two-week period of communication with him by e-mail and telephone. Eventually they met face-to-face and the author was soon won over; a mutually trusting relationship developed between the two. There was no doubt that the man was legitimate. He was an authentic ambassador who had undeniably been a guest of the Verdants aboard the *Goodwill*, the mother ship stationed in the vicinity of the Earth.

The man, whom the author refers to by the pseudonym Louis Winslow, was an integral figure in the Verdants' plans for contact, designated to play a major role. Of course, this was a secret part of his life that he had shared with no one. After the postponement, Louis had some blunt discussions with the Verdants about the possibilities for an early resumption of the contact plans. Although the Verdants could not provide any specific timetable, they did provide him with a realistic assessment of the current human condition and the effects it was having on their mission.

Louis admitted to the author during one of their face-to-face sessions that he came away from the discussions with the Verdants in a deep funk. He was despondent and felt like someone who had suffered a terrible psychological whipping. In addition, he was convinced that humanity was doomed, that the world would not recover from its madness, and that the Verdants would ultimately give up on the human race. After all, it was no secret among the ambassadors that the Verdants had indicated having seen such meltdowns before in other civilizations.

In essence, Louis explained that he had been in a state of grief. Not only was he fearful for the future of the human race, but on a more personal and selfish level he was mourning his own lost opportunity, the chance to play a key role in the most significant moment in human history. His personal life also had been a mess, he admitted. And even if contact plans were renewed in his lifetime, it would be necessary to recruit almost a whole new slate of ambassadors because many original ones would have died while others would be too aged to take on the burden required, he said.

Hopeless, alone, unhappy, and dispirited, he accepted an offer by the Verdants to participate in a "sabbatical," an offer tendered because of the high esteem and regard in which the Verdants held him. He had poured himself into his tasks on behalf of the contact project with energy, enthusiasm, dedication, and plain old hard work. And it was appreciated.

After wrapping up his personal and business affairs one day in 2002, Louis ended a meeting with his lawyer, walked out into the sunshine, handed his expensive watch to a panhandler—he wouldn't need it where he was going—and disappeared from the face of the Earth—literally.

And then Louis dropped a bombshell on the author.

Louis revealed that he had just returned from a four-year odyssey in which he lived among the Verdants on two colonized planets in the Milky Way galaxy!

But if Louis had left our home planet full of despair and hopelessness, the man sitting before the author was light-years removed from his previous self. This new person was robust in every sense of the word in body and spirit. He admitted that he had been transformed, and he related a fascinating tale of hope and personal rejuvenation.

Despite the vast distances involved, and thanks to the flicker drive technology, Louis spent the overwhelming majority of time in those four years living among the Verdants and an insignificant time in transit. Yes, he experienced extreme culture shock as well as "future shock" in his new environment, but it would be better described as a stunning experience of pure joy and awe-inspiring discovery rather than of confusion and disorientation.

The astonishment of being among a race of people living in complete global harmony and peace touched him at the core of his being. Such a utopian civilization has been a wispy fantasy for human dreamers since time immemorial. Louis wondered if the contemporary human mind is even capable of evoking images of a world free of drug abuse, squalid poverty, suicide, violence, homelessness, hunger, alcoholism, mental illness, and other diseases, and all of the other forms of wretchedness that afflict the human condition.

A civilization that is more than 200 million years older than ours is quite literally unimaginable. Understandably, Louis made no attempt to define it. He merely spoke soothingly of the little—but miraculous—things that he could comprehend and appreciate.

Imagine a bustling city of millions of people—and no noise, no sound beyond the low ambient hum of countless quiet conversations. No police sirens, no construction racket, no roar of traffic, no clatter of jackhammers, not a single blaring vehicle horn. No panhandlers, no raucous groups of rowdy street toughs, no trash-littered streets.

Visualize the breathtaking grandeur of magnificent architecture surrounded by unlimited open space framed by colorful plants and trees under a brilliant bluish sky. Envision the same city at night, softly lit by muted lighting and the heavenly illumination of two moons, one occupying ten percent of the night sky accompanied by a much smaller and fainter sister, marching high above across the firmament.

And he could barely fathom a society that had absolutely no need for prisons, insurance policies, locks and keys, police, food stamps, armies, battered women's shelters, juries, child welfare agencies, charities, ad infinitum.

As time passed during the four years that he spent living among the Verdants, he said that he actually could feel himself being quietly and manifestly transformed, finally becoming aware that for the first time in his life he was actually getting in touch with himself.

After many hours of marathon sessions over a period of several days during which Louis related his four-year experiences, it came as no surprise to the author when Louis proclaimed that he had discovered his soul.

Louis also brought back news regarding the Verdants' considerations about renewing the Contact Project, including an item that directly affects the author's role if any new plan were to be carried out.

But that is a story for another time.